POWER PLAY

POWER PLAY

How Video Games Can Save the World

Asi Burak and
Laura Parker

ST. MARTIN'S PRESS New York

www.stmartins.com

Designed by Ellen Cipriano

Library of Congress Cataloging-in-Publication Data is available from the Library of Congress.

ISBN 9781250089335 (hardcover)
ISBN 9781250089342 (ebook)

Our books may be purchased in bulk for promotional, educational, or business use. Please contact your local bookseller or the Macmillan Corporate and Premium Sales Department at 1-800-221-7945, extension 5442, or by e-mail at MacmillanSpecialMarkets@macmillan.com.

First Edition: January 2017

10 9 8 7 6 5 4 3 2 1

ASI: *To the women in my life,*
   Britta, Amalia, and Danielle.

LAURA: *For Darryn.*

Contents

PART III: FROM THE LAB TO THE SCREEN

PART IV: THE TOOLS OF A NEW GENERATION

Introduction

The year he turned 30, the comic book artist Art Spiegelman embarked on his most ambitious project yet. He figured the best artists die young, preferably in motorcycle accidents, so he'd better put his remaining time to good use. "I needed to justify being alive," he told us recently, speaking on the phone from his studio in SoHo, Manhattan.

He imagined a comic book that would read like the kind of book you'd need a bookmark for, in which he'd attempt to explore his feelings about his at times strenuous relationship with his father, Vladek, a Holocaust survivor. But he never imagined the impact the book could have.

As publisher (along with his wife, Francoise) of the comics anthology *RAW* (1980–1991), Spiegelman knew comic strips that explored personal, even taboo topics; many of the artists featured in the anthology stretched the medium to its limits. In fact, you could say the anthology itself was based on the assumption that comics had possibilities as limitless as those of books. *RAW* was aimed at a small crowd of artists who felt the same way, and since Spiegelman was at the center of this underground scene, he didn't see his new work as provocative—just highly ambitious. He was simply aiming to do "the hardest thing imaginable."

In 1986, Spiegelman published the first volume of *Maus: A Survivor's Tale: My Father Bleeds History*, tackling a subject that's almost impossible to address even in more traditional art forms. The comic book chronicles the experiences of Spiegelman's father, a Polish Jew, and his mother, from the years leading up to World War II through their liberation from the Nazi concentration camp in Auschwitz. Jews are drawn as mice, Germans as cats, and (non-Jewish) Poles as pigs.

Spiegelman's expectations were low. Most of the publishers he'd approached had rejected the work, writing long and thoughtful responses with the same bottom line. Finally, Pantheon Books agreed to publish the book, but not before they advised him to hide somewhere in the countryside and avoid reading reviews. They needn't have worried: the response to *Maus* was thunderous. It has gone on to sell over a million copies in the United States alone and been translated into 30 languages. Spiegelman went on to win a Pulitzer Prize, among many other awards. Suddenly, PhD students around the world were writing academic papers about *Maus*.

Slowly, comic books began to shift from the pulp fiction shelf to nonfiction or politics. People began to refer to comic books as "graphic novels." Works like *Palestine, Persepolis, From Hell*, and

V for Vendetta were celebrated as ushering in a new era for the art form. It became fashionable to read comic books on the subway.

Spiegelman said he never intended *Maus* to "educate." He rejected the idea of the book being read by, or taught to, kids—simply because it was not intended for them but for adults instead. He regards art as thorny, unsettling—and certainly not well-intentioned. Today, his resolve has softened somewhat. He says the Pulitzer gave him, and comic books, a "cloak of respectability." It encouraged other artists to follow in his footsteps.

Speaking to Spiegelman, one hears the story of how an artist changed the boundaries of a medium—even if inadvertently. He's an inspiration to those of us looking to do the same.

ALTHOUGH THERE ARE MANY parallels between comic books and video games, the cultural popularity of video games has spread much faster than that of comic books—the current Marvel movie franchises notwithstanding. In the summer of 2015, New York's Madison Square Garden hosted its first video game tournament in front of 20,000 viewers; Amazon bought the live-streaming video game service Twitch for $970 million; and leading museums from around the world, including the Museum of Modern Art in New York and the Smithsonian, in Washington, DC, have added video games to their permanent collections.

Contemporary video games no longer fit into a handful of prescribed genres—shooters, adventure games, role-playing games, and so on. We have blockbuster mobile games like Angry Birds and Candy Crush. We also have independent games, innovative projects that subvert popular gaming genres by giving an artistic and even personal feeling: among them Braid, Journey, Gone Home, and Telltale Games' The Walking Dead.

But to us, there is no genre of games more compelling than "games for change": those created not simply to entertain, but to promote positive social change and help solve the thorniest problems in the world.

This book is about the pioneers behind these games—artists, scientists, journalists, even a former Supreme Court justice. Their work has addressed a broad range of pressing issues, from global conflict resolution and women's rights to cancer treatment.

And yet, despite this momentous progress, it's not uncommon to hear people dismiss video games as hopelessly violent, as just for kids, as a bad influence and a giant waste of time.

With this book, we hope to settle this debate once and for all. Some of the stories you'll read are about very successful games; others are not. We haven't glossed over the many speed bumps that come with the journey. Yet the men and women featured in this book have persevered to remake the medium and, in turn, pave the way for a new generation of engineers and designers who understand its limitless potential.

Other art forms have addressed social issues for decades. We've all watched movies like *Schindler's List* and *Spotlight*; gone to galleries to see political or activist art; and embraced novelists who show us what it's like to walk in someone else's shoes. With video games, the opportunity to see life from another point of view is even greater, because games' inherent interactivity promotes agency and a new type of immersive experience.

The new generation of young consumers is both socially alert and deeply engaged. We know millennials volunteer with non-profit organizations, raise money for social causes, and donate to charities. If we combine this strong interest with where these young consumers already spend their time (hint: online), games for change prove to be a natural fit.

It's taken over a decade to get to this point. Game creators, funders, and consumers have evolved together, experimenting with media conventions and vocabulary—and with business models—to see which ones best make and measure impact. This book chronicles the journey so far, but it also looks ahead, to see how much more can be done. For organizations and individuals who would like to get involved, we foresee great opportunities for impact as well as financial success.

The book is split up into four parts. In Part I, "Not Playing Around Anymore" (Chapters 1–3), we make our way from Israel in the '70s to modern day Pittsburgh to chronicle the journey of a little game about peace that helped kickstart the games for change movement; we spend some quality time with former Supreme Court justice Sandra Day O'Connor to tell the story of her nationally lauded iCivics gaming platform, whose aim is to turn all young Americans into informed political thinkers; and we finish up in Macon, Georgia, to witness a unique experiment in real world social gaming to build bridges between strangers and isolated communities.

In Part II, "From Jeddah to Nairobi" (Chapters 4–5), we tell the story of a Saudi Arabian prince that goes against tradition and stereotypes, and finish up in New York, where Pulitzer-winning authors Nick Kristof and Sheryl WuDunn's global Half the Sky Movement got the world to pay attention to the plight of underprivileged women from around the world. (Video games were involved, of course.)

In Part III, "From the Lab to the Screen" (Chapters 6–8), our protagonists are on a scientific mission, creating games to solve acute scientific or medical problems. There's Re-Mission, a game that helps young cancer patients stick to their treatment, and Project Evo, the video game that might one day be played by prescription. We also look at innovative platforms like Zooniverse, where budding amateur scientists from around the world chronicle undiscovered corners of the universe using simple game design.

In the final part, "The Tools of a New Generation" (Chapters 9–10), we explore the promise of virtual reality to address social and political issues with unprecedented immersion, and see what the next generation of game makers have in store for the future.

We're well aware that we've focused mostly on the positives. But that's what this book is about: celebrating the artists, designers, and entrepreneurs championing video games as a force for good.

So: Don't turn your console off and go to bed. Sit up and play.

PART I

NOT PLAYING AROUND ANYMORE

*Video Games that Enhance
Our Understanding of the
World, and Each Other.*

1.

A Little Game about Peace

(THE STORY OF PEACEMAKER)

t's morning rush hour in Jerusalem. A pink haze hangs low over the streets. Cars, buses, and pedestrians jostle for space. Bleary-eyed schoolchildren trundle past shopkeepers rolling up heavy steel doors.

A man boards a bus. He stands beside early morning shoppers, retired old ladies with oversized canvas shopping bags, and soldiers on their way to the training academy. There are children, too, off to school on the other side of town. The man waits until the bus is full, until passengers are pushing up against the windows and doors. Only then does he open his jacket and detonate the explosive strapped to his chest.

There's a flash of white-hot light and a low-pitched rumble, like distant thunder. The flames spread quickly. There's a hole where the street used to be, its edges charred and smoky, glass raining down like confetti. The bus itself is barely visible in the smoke, its crumpled metal insides twisted and poking skyward. The ground beneath it is slippery with oil, tar, and blood.

Sirens wail in the distance. A crowd slowly forms; some people reach down into the hole, searching for survivors. Others simply watch, praying that the bodies scattered at their feet don't belong to friends or relatives. Police and paramedics arrive. They work silently, the routine all too familiar. Yellow police tape goes up. People are told to go home. The camera crews arrive last, training their lenses on the growing pile of black body bags on the side of the road. By midday, news of the attack is everywhere. Nineteen are dead, and more than fifty seriously injured.

We zoom out. It's February 2007, and Major General Danny Yatom, the former head of the Mossad, Israel's national intelligence agency, is sitting at a mahogany desk playing a video game. A warning message pops up on his screen. It reads, "Hamas claims responsibility for a suicide bombing in Jerusalem. How will you respond?"

Yatom is wearing a black suit and a burgundy tie. Behind him is the Israeli flag; to his left is his "power wall"—framed photos of Yatom with various world leaders. A news crew from Israel's Channel 2 is standing behind the desk, filming him for that night's evening news.[1] The violent scene described above—a Palestinian suicide bomber detonating a device packed with ball bearings on a crowded bus in the middle of Jerusalem—is the game's opening gambit.

Off-camera, a young reporter tells Yatom that the game requires him to choose a side before he can play. "Do you wish to play as the Israeli leader, or the Palestinian leader?"

Yatom does not hesitate: "The Israeli." The game presents him with his first task: responding to the suicide attack.

"It is clear to me that I need to seek out the terrorists' nest and strike back," he says out loud, not diverting his eyes from the screen. The camera follows him as he sends army troops in for a ground assault. Satisfied by the outcome of the attack, he presses on. "This time I am going for the leadership of Hamas," he says excitedly. "Let's order a targeted Apache strike."

The reporter interjects from across the room, "Remember, General, this is a game designed to demonstrate the complexity of the Israeli-Palestinian conflict: too much aggression and you might lose."

Yatom reconsiders. "Fine. I will move to diplomacy. I will reach out to the Palestinian president and seek collaboration." After a few minutes, he doubles back. "Wait. I am going to demand—to force, in fact—military action against the terrorists." The reporter protests, but Yatom pushes on. The screen begins to flash an angry red. A message pops up informing Yatom that his decision has led to a new Palestinian uprising. Game over.

"'You have lost,'" Yatom reads. He looks up at the camera, smiling. "I lost because the computer decided I lost. In my opinion, I did all the right things."

Yatom was playing PeaceMaker, a simulation of the Israeli-Palestinian conflict, developed by Asi Burak and a small team of developers at Carnegie Mellon University (CMU) in Pittsburgh. The game had just been published on Amazon and was getting a lot of attention from the press—in the United States, where Asi lived, as well as in Israel, his home country.

When Asi first began work on PeaceMaker, he didn't know

what kind of game it would be, or who would play it. All he knew was that video games were finally being taken seriously. People everywhere, from public schools to the United Nations, were looking at games as a new way to teach and inspire the younger generations.

A few days after PeaceMaker's release, Asi received a call from the largest television network in Israel. The network's representatives told him they wanted to test the game out on Major General Yatom, who, at the time, was running for the Israeli Labor Party leadership. Sure, Asi said. There's probably no better way to see if the game actually works than having a leading politician play it on national television.

PeaceMaker asks players to navigate a series of events and hostilities—like the suicide bombing on the bus—through a combination of military intervention and diplomacy. How, for example, should Israel have responded to the bus bombing that inspired the game's opening scene? The scene was based on a real event, and in real life, Israel launched a raid on the West Bank. Was it justified? Was it effective? Might there have been a different, more diplomatic course of action that would have yielded a better result?

Serious games, or "games for change," are often criticized for being too earnest or preachy. PeaceMaker is an exception. Asi and his team used real news footage to illustrate the attacks and events in the game. This had never been done before. The goal was simple: to show people, especially young people, that not all games involving violence have to be made purely for entertainment—that their interactivity could be used to create empathy and provide insight, even into a problem as entrenched and complex as the

Israeli-Palestinian conflict; and, more fundamentally, that violence doesn't end when you turn the computer off.

As an Israeli who had spent the last three years researching the conflict, Asi recognized the power of an experience that could safely and realistically put players in someone else's shoes.

In the same broadcast for which Yatom played PeaceMaker for the cameras, the reporter asked Asi what *he* thought about Yatom's decisions in the game. "What happened to Yatom essentially proves that the game is realistic," Asi told the reporter. "This is exactly what's been happening to the State of Israel for decades. It's the same cycle, the same actions that lead to the same depressing results."

The reporter mused, "In PeaceMaker, you can eventually reach peace. So perhaps the game is not so realistic after all."

ASI GREW UP IN a middle-class suburb of Tel Aviv. His university-educated parents took great pains to give him as much creative freedom as he could handle. For him, that meant drawing. He drew a lot as a kid, and somewhere along the way, it was decided that he had a talent for it. His kindergarten teacher used to corner his parents during parent-teacher nights to show them his drawings. "Have you seen Asi's latest?" she'd say, thrusting a pile of crudely drawn clowns at them.

Over time, Asi stopped drawing clowns and started drawing tanks. He was too young to register what was happening around him, but he saw the planes overhead and the tanks in the streets. Plus, everyone talked about it constantly. No one in Israel discussed sports or entertainment or culture with as much zeal as when they talked about "the situation." "As a nation, the conflict defined us," Asi says today.

In primary school, Asi's teacher asked the class whether they believed Israel should return the occupied territories to the Palestinians. "No," they chorused. "We were attacked and won the war, didn't we? Why should we have to give anything back?" When Asi related this to his parents, his father was taken aback. "Why do you seem so sure?" he asked Asi. "I don't know," Asi replied. "But it's just fair, isn't it?" Asi's father explained that things weren't so simple—that each side had its own reasons for wanting what they did. That was the first time Asi had heard anyone express that idea. His father was certainly a liberal, but that was not uncommon at the time. Asi began to question his feelings. "I was Israeli, but did that always make me right?"

In high school, Asi decided to study Arabic—an unusual choice for a middle-class kid from Tel Aviv with good grades. A year later, the military showed up at his school to recruit for the following year's compulsory service programs. In Israel, compulsory military service for men begins when they are 18 and lasts three years. A few of Asi's teachers recommended him for an elite program, and when the army found out he was studying Arabic, they immediately scheduled the eight-hour entrance test.

Asi passed the test, but his parents worried. It turned out he had to do a seven-month preliminary course in addition to the three years of mandatory service, and the course required a whole bunch of secret assignments. The army needed his parents' signature, so they sent the head of the course to Asi's house. He explained that the elite program wasn't as simple as the mandatory military service—that there was much more at stake. Recruits would be dealing with life-and-death situations. Because of the sensitive nature of the information they would have access to, failing a mission could mean prison.

Asi began the course the following week. "We studied morning and night, only going home on the weekends. We couldn't say anything about what we were doing or even where we were." On the surface, the work the recruits were doing was similar to that of the National Security Agency (NSA)—collecting and analyzing data. "Say, for example, that we knew of ten ultra-sensitive emails between two heads of state, but for whatever reason we couldn't get our hands on all ten, just half. My job would be to read those five emails and fill in the gaps. It was analytics, mostly, but it also required me to use the creative part of my brain quite a lot, which I enjoyed."

Once the actual program began, though, things quickly changed. Suddenly, Asi knew so much more than what regular people did. He'd pick up a newspaper and immediately recognize what was truth and what was speculation. He couldn't talk about any of it, of course, but it made him feel powerful. "It was as if I'd suddenly gained X-ray vision."

Slowly, his feelings about what he was doing began to change. As Israeli soldiers, the recruits were constantly fed the idea that they were fighting the good fight, saving lives on a daily basis. But after a few years behind the scenes, some of them had begun to realize that it was mostly thrust and parry, a never-ending circle of violence.

At times, what they were doing felt almost like a game. For one thing, it was nearly always about winning or losing. One operation Asi remembers involved targeting a high-level meeting of militants in South Lebanon. The operation involved months of preparation, total secrecy, and classified reports that only a handful of soldiers in the whole Israeli army could see. Everything went smoothly, and Asi's teammates were exhilarated. "There was actual applause in our bunker," he says.

Sometimes, lives were indeed saved, and people were kept safe. But major events like the Oslo Accords and the 1991 Iraqi surprise attack on Kuwait proved that seismic change often doesn't happen on the military level. The most important breakthroughs are political and often hard to predict. War with Hamas or Hezbollah, on the other hand, can feel like a constant loop. As soon as one problem is eliminated, another pops up in its place. "We'd successfully take out a target or disarm a militant leader, and someone bigger and even more dangerous would replace them," Asi says. "I knew a lot and understood a lot, but to what end? Nothing changed."

After five years, in which he became an officer, and then a captain, Asi had had enough. He quit the army and applied to the best art school in Israel, the Bezalel Academy of Arts and Design. After graduating, he worked in advertising and in the emerging mobile-app market, but he felt restless. "It was almost like I tried to take a break from the army, and get back to normal. But in Israel there is no normal."

Although he was working in an emerging industry, Asi couldn't get excited. Everything he did felt meaningless. He didn't yet know how, but he knew he had to find a way to use his talent to make an impact—he just wasn't sure what kind.

In 2003, during a late-night session of scouring job boards, Asi was suddenly taken with the idea of studying abroad. He began looking at grad programs and hit upon Carnegie Mellon University. One sentence describing CMU's new Entertainment Technology Center jumped out: "Video games are a largely untapped medium for expression."

Even though he'd played games nonstop as a kid in the '80s, on his Atari and then the Apple IIe, he hadn't touched one since.

But could games be the next big thing? When Asi saw that sentence on CMU's site, something clicked. It spoke to his experience: design, the army intelligence service, the old love for games, and his passion for politics. Here, perhaps, was his chance to do something that mattered.

He began reading about the pioneering work being done with games at places like MIT Media Lab and New York University. He bought books about virtual communities and online avatars, like Janet Murray's *Hamlet on the Holodeck*. It was instantly clear that this was powerful stuff, and he had only just scratched the surface. But what astounded Asi the most was how far technology had come since his game-playing days—and how much the meaning of the words "video game" had changed.

Ultimately, he saw an opportunity. "Imagine working on an art form that most people don't yet fully appreciate, but that you know will grow into something incredible one day," he says. "A medium that many people consider shallow, or violent, but whose potential to teach and transform is in fact limitless."

A week later, Asi enrolled in the Carnegie Mellon program and spent the next six months catching up. He bought a new PlayStation console and locked himself in the house, getting reacquainted with everything from Doom to Hitman. The 3D graphics were astounding, yet almost nothing grabbed him emotionally or intellectually. He still somehow preferred the old text adventure games he'd played growing up. Video games certainly *looked* amazing now, but what about their storytelling power? Could a game both be visually engaging and successfully communicate a deeper message?

One game series that led Asi to hope was Hideo Kojima's Metal Gear Solid. Even though it was designed as a common third-person shooter game, there were moments when it was clear that the designers wanted to surprise players, or throw them off balance. An example is when the protagonist is confronted with the ghosts of everyone he's killed in the game, or when the game begins addressing the player directly: "Stop playing games, put the joystick away."

He thought, "If even just 5 percent of the game was so thought-provoking, couldn't we make a game that's *all about* challenging our assumptions and making us rethink our values?"

That's how PeaceMaker was born. A video game about the Israeli-Palestinian conflict would challenge players to make the same kinds of decisions that the real people in charge are making every day. The game would certainly be provocative. Nothing quite like that had been attempted before. And who better to create it than a kid who'd grown up in the middle of the conflict?

In August 2004, Asi moved to Pittsburgh. Since he didn't want to walk into CMU on his first day and say, "Hey guys, I already know what I want to spend the next two years doing, and you're going to love it," he took some time to adjust. He got to know his lecturers—among them Jesse Schell, Don Marinelli, and the late Randy Pausch, whose 2007 lecture at Carnegie Mellon reflecting on his terminal cancer diagnosis became a YouTube sensation.[2] There was also the fact that Asi was ten years older than everyone else in his class.

Each semester, the faculty assigned the class specific projects. Often, the projects were sponsored—say, an interactive game for Disney to complement the entertainment giant's new television show, or an interactive installation for the Children's Museum of Pittsburgh. Students could also pitch their own projects to the faculty, but the chance of success was very low: on average, the faculty only accepted 10 percent of the pitches they saw each year. The reason given was that they didn't have the resources to spare for more. Sponsored projects were, of course, paid for, and the final product would be good publicity for CMU; approving student-run projects meant CMU had to invest its own resources in ideas that could fail.

The semester before Asi came to CMU, a group of 12 students pitched an idea for a large-scale 3D game about zombies. The project kept growing in scope each semester until, finally, it fell apart. Come graduation, the group hadn't finished even a quarter of what they were supposed to. The project was a big red flag for the faculty, and everyone in the program spoke of it in hushed tones—the urban legend of Asi's master's class. "Oh, you want to pitch your own project? Be careful man—you don't want to end up like the zombie guys."

During his first week at CMU, Asi met another student, a stern-looking kid named Ross Popoff. He was 23 and very interested in what Asi had to say about Israel, Palestine, and a game that "could change the world." He said he wanted to help Asi get it off the ground. The pair began working on a pitch for the university board.

Ross and Asi quickly became inseparable. "We were best friends; we sat together in class, ate together, and spent most of our downtime refining the pitch for PeaceMaker," Asi says.

They knew the idea was good, but convincing the faculty would take some work. The pitching process itself was complicated: one initial pitch, then two follow-up pitches. Each time, students had to demonstrate that the idea had progressed significantly.

Ross and Asi went in for the initial pitch about a month after they first met. It was a tense morning. They'd decided to wear suits and ties, except that Asi didn't actually know how to tie a tie. (Hardly anyone wears suits in Israel—it's hot, and opportunities to wear a suit don't come very often.) Ross helped Asi with the tie in the men's room, five minutes before the presentation was due to begin. It was 10:00 a.m., and other candidates were already waiting. Asi couldn't help noticing that none of them had bothered to dress up.

Asi and Ross were finally called inside a big, airy boardroom with tall windows, where ten faculty members sat at a long table. There was nothing else in the room—not even curtains on the windows. For some reason, it reminded Asi of the film *Flashdance* (which, coincidentally, was also filmed in Pittsburgh), particularly the final scene—probably all the more so because he'd brought his own CD player.

"What's going on?" Ross whispered to Asi as they began setting up. If the pair had hoped for banal chitchat to break the ice, they clearly weren't going to get it. Everyone at the table stared pointedly at Ross as he plugged in the CD player and set up the PowerPoint slides on the projector. He had compiled a soundtrack with some of the sounds Asi and Ross imagined they'd have in the game—machine guns, airplanes, and an Israeli siren that warns residents of an imminent rocket attack. They'd also brought ten blindfolds, crudely torn the night before from a single white sheet.

Asi picked up the blindfolds and walked over to the table. "Could you please put on these blindfolds?" he said, trying not to look any of the faculty members directly in the eye. Some shifted in their seats and exchanged confused glances, but one by one, they did as they were asked. "I expected at least one of them to say *something*, even a wisecrack, but no one did," Asi says.

Asi looked at Ross, who shrugged. They hit play. For two minutes, the sounds of a war zone filled the room. Then Ross asked the faculty members to remove their blindfolds. The first thing they saw was an old Palestinian woman, tears streaking her face, arms outstretched toward a group of Israeli soldiers. The next slide was of a suicide bus bombing in Jerusalem. Next, a child standing in front of tanks in Gaza. When the slideshow ended, Ross started talking.

"This will be a video game about negotiation, not about fighting or destruction. It will show the horrors of the conflict between Israel and Palestine, but it will also attempt to engage the player in the journey toward peace. The road there will be filled with tough decision making, with life-or-death situations."

Asi cut in. "Mainstream video games have been both too violent and too shallow for too long. Around 87 percent of contemporary games include violent content. We want to create a game that will be about a real-life conflict. This is no fantasy world."

"We'll recruit a team of talented game programmers, artists and designers, and we hope to have this completed within the year," Ross continued.

Asi looked at the clock. Two minutes left. He and Ross stood in silence, looking at the faculty members. Asi wasn't sure if they realized that he and Ross had finished; he was just about to speak again when Randy Pausch shifted in his seat and said: "This game is . . ." he paused. "Well, it is widely out of scope."

Ross and Asi stood dumbfounded. They were sure they'd won the faculty over. Randy spoke again. "It's a bold idea, but it seems to me that you don't really have a good plan for executing it." Another faculty member on the panel spoke up. "Can you tell me in three sentences what you're trying to do?"

Asi and Ross mumbled something about emotion, about the real world, about a video game that would finally attempt to show players a perspective on true events. It was a vague reply, at best. There was a lot left out, things they hadn't even talked about yet, such as: Who exactly was this game for? Israelis and Palestinians? Americans? Schoolchildren? Or mainstream gamers?

Finally, just as Asi thought they were going to be kicked out, Randy said, "Come back in a month, and be ready to show us something more concrete."

Asi and Ross set about recruiting students to help get started on the game. Most students they talked to seemed excited by the idea. CMU was one of those places that recognized the importance— and validity—of games early on. Asi began lobbying the faculty, like a senator on the campaign trail. He set up one-on-one meetings with each person who'd sat at that long table and asked them for advice and feedback. "I wanted them to see that I was extremely invested in this thing."

After talking to other students in their class, Asi and Ross settled on a programmer named Eric Keylor. It was Eric who convinced them that their best chance of success with the game was to use 2D simulation, not 3D. A 3D game would require a huge amount of work to pull off successfully, and no one would be interested in the ideas if they were too busy mocking the bad graphics. With 2D, Asi and Ross at least had a chance to focus on communicating a central message without having to worry too much about rendering backgrounds and character animations. Asi liked to think of it as a Sim City for peace, the kind of game in which players can build physical infrastructure and watch how it impacts the virtual environment.

The team spent the next few weeks refining the concept for the game, coming up with some crude art and a few of the key choices that players in the game would have to make. Asi also did some research into other games with serious themes, or serious games, as they were called, to see what the competition was. What he discovered was that the timing for their project couldn't have been better. When he first arrived at CMU, in 2004, serious games had been around for a year or two, but under the radar and with limited impact. Many projects aimed for government and military applications, building on the success of games like America's Army, developed and used by the US Army beginning in 2002 to recruit young men and women. But there was a feeling that serious games would one day be as financially successful as entertainment games and would be used in education, training, and a number of other professional contexts.

This optimism was further bolstered by the arrival of "news games," which took serious, newsworthy topics as their subject. The two leaders in this field back then were Gonzalo Frasca, the creator of an iconic game called September 12th,[3] and Ian Bogost, who often experimented with the form as a designer and later wrote a textbook, *Newsgames: Journalism at Play*. September 12th, created in response to 9/11, was a smart, sharp commentary that played for no longer than five minutes. It was less like a game and more like an interactive cartoon, one that featured a village full of people, made up of militants (who hold guns) and civilians. The only element players could control was a crosshairs, except that whatever weapon the crosshairs belonged to was extremely inefficient and inaccurate, meaning that even if players aimed for the militants, a whole bunch of civilians would end up dying as well. Each civilian who was shot immediately turned into a militant. "Naming it September 12th was provocative—there is no way to win the war on terror but to create more terror," Asi says. "Looking at that now, you can understand how prophetic it is." One member of the faculty at CMU told Asi that if he could pull off something as polished as September 12th, he'd have a winner on his hands.

The best-known serious games at the time were A Force More Powerful, Darfur Is Dying, and Food Force. A Force More Powerful was a fairly complex simulation of nonviolent resistance movements; Food Force was a polished 3D game, created with funding from the UN, that has since been translated into multiple languages; and Darfur Is Dying broke ground by being associated with a big brand (MTV), reaching two million players and including a direct call to action—players were invited to write letters to Congress about the issue, a new concept in games at the time.

Asi took all of this information with him to the second pitch in front of the faculty. This time, the atmosphere was visibly warmer. For one thing, Asi and Ross weren't as terrified as they'd been the first time, because they already knew to expect the worst. For another, people were actually smiling.

Asi and Ross talked through the progress they'd made, and Randy was again the first to speak. "We are going to give you the go-ahead to continue," he said. "It is not that we don't have our doubts still, but you are clearly motivated to succeed here." Other faculty members cut in with advice and tips. "We are always here to help," said Josh Yelon, a nerdy computer science teacher who later volunteered to be one of the project's mentors. "But you'll need to do the heavy lifting. To be honest, I don't envy you."

Ross and Asi brought on Tim Sweeney, another kid in the class, to be the official game designer. Tim had a long, unkempt red beard and bad sleeping patterns. He worked on the game in his spare time, and preferred to keep out of the spotlight. Ross eventually left the project due to disagreements over the development strategy, and Asi and Tim moved into their own office. They dedicated every spare second to PeaceMaker. They made a digital demo—a modest prototype of the Israeli version of the game. (The idea to include a Palestinian point of view came later.) At that stage, they were simply exploring which values would come into conflict for an Israeli leader. How did security measures taken by Israel immediately affect the Palestinians' quality of life? And how did concessions to the Palestinians make Israelis feel less safe?

To explore that core tension, Tim first designed a paper-based board game, and then a dice game. Once the premise was tested and validated by some of Tim and Asi's fellow classmates and a few of the faculty staff, the duo made a rough text version of the game. There was a map and a very crude interface with some icons and a few key decision points for the player. It was at this stage that Asi and Tim decided to use real-world footage. Using such footage was a little risky; at that time, no other game had tried it. "We thought, it's one thing to draw a suicide bomb; it's quite another to see the real thing," Asi says.

Progress was slow. But then, something happened that pushed PeaceMaker from a small student project into the cornerstone of the serious games movement.

Soon after Asi began work on PeaceMaker, word got out in the Pittsburgh press that students at CMU were working on a video game about the Israeli–Palestinian conflict. A few local papers came to interview Asi, Ross, and Tim. Then Al Jazeera sent an Arabic-speaking crew all the way from Qatar to do a story.[4] Finally, the *New York Times* ran a front-page story[5] in the Sunday arts section on a new wave of video games set to change the world. The accompanying photo was a half-page screenshot of Peace-Maker under the headline, "Saving the world, one video game at a time."

Don Marinelli, who had co-founded CMU's Entertainment Technology Center with Randy, bought 100 copies of the paper when the story came out. Asi remembers him running down the hall to his and Tim's office that day, shouting, "Some people would give their right arm to get this type of coverage!" Asi also remembers what Don said next: "Guys, you need to start making sure this is real."

They were hearing this a lot. On one hand, the faculty was happy to be getting so much outside attention. On the other hand, they were worried about having another zombie game on their hands, only this time under a national spotlight. They didn't want this thing to fizzle out and die. They wanted a success story. And PeaceMaker was far from that. The demo was good, but it was nothing like the real thing. The code was still crude and the scenarios in the game half-baked. Both Don and Randy began stopping by the office almost daily, offering feedback and checking up on the game's progress.

The problem was that Asi and Tim were really familiar with only one side of the conflict. Obviously, Asi knew a lot about Israel and its involvement in the matter, but the game needed help when it came to representing the Palestinian side of the issue. So Asi asked around the faculty, and someone pointed him to Laurie Eisenberg, a CMU history professor who specialized in the conflict. Eisenberg invited Asi and Tim to sit in on some of her classes, and after a while the two PeaceMaker designers realized that this would be the perfect environment in which to test a prototype of the game. Eisenberg always discussed the conflict with her class—why not introduce them to a game about it? Asi and Tim spent a few weeks making a playable version of PeaceMaker and brought it to one of Eisenberg's classes. At first, the students didn't know what to make of the game, but they soon got the hang of it. As they played, Eisenberg would ask them questions like "How did it make you feel?" and "What did you learn about the Israeli side?"

Soon, Asi and Tim began to hear some unexpected things. One student said she'd learned more about the Israeli-Palestinian conflict by playing PeaceMaker for an hour than from everything she'd read or seen in newspapers and on television. That was the first, but not the last, time Asi and Tim heard this.

After that, Asi and Tim began testing the game all the time: in Eisenberg's class, even in high schools around Pittsburgh, including a local Jewish school. They were now trying to answer design questions like whether or not to have a scoring system; how do you quantify something as serious as war? Would a score undermine the complexity of the issue? How do you put a number on human suffering?

Meanwhile, word of the game was spreading. When people outside the university—stakeholders, prospective clients—asked the faculty to show them a range of CMU student projects, the faculty always chose PeaceMaker. "We quickly became the go-to project." This is how Asi first met Bing Gordon.

Gordon, the chief creative officer at Electronic Arts at the time, had come to CMU as a guest lecturer. He and Randy were good friends, and after the lecture he asked Randy to show him some of the projects by the master's students. Randy brought him to Asi and Tim's office. The two students were in the middle of a design session. The office was cramped and had no windows. Bing is a big guy. When he appeared in the doorway, his body cast an enormous shadow over Asi and Tim's desk.

"You guys got something you want to show me?" he asked them. "That's what I love about Bing, he was a no-bullshit kind of guy," Asi says. They gave him the pitch—by this stage they'd done it so many times they could recite it in their sleep—and waited for his reaction.

He started firing off questions. What's unique about this game? Why does it matter?

"It's the first video game about a real-life conflict," Asi fired back. "No," Bing said flatly. "What's unique about your game is not that it's the first game about a real-life conflict. It's that it's the first game about peace."

And with that, Bing had found the specific magic in Asi and Tim's nebulous idea—the essence of what they were trying to achieve. He was in their office for only 20 minutes, but by the time he left, Asi and Tim finally knew what to say when people asked who exactly this game was meant for and what it was about. It was a game about peace: for Americans, Palestinians, and Israeli youth. Simple as that.

Before Bing left, Asi asked for permission to keep him updated on their progress. Bing said sure. It was Bing whom Asi emailed when he was having doubts about whether to continue with the press coverage in the face of not actually having much game to show. "The life cycle of a game is long," Bing wrote back. "If it's a good story, they'll write about it again and again and again. Kiss the press and be happy this is happening. This isn't your only shot. Be grateful and use it in every way possible."

A few months after Bing Gordon's visit, Eisenberg came up with another opportunity. CMU had a sister branch in Qatar, and Eisenberg had been invited to teach classes to students there via video link. "What if we took PeaceMaker to Qatar?" she asked Asi and Tim. The faculty seemed to agree that it was a good, though bold, idea, and suddenly, Asi and Tim were packing their bags. "We're going to Qatar!" they shouted to each other in the halls.

In Qatar, they spoke to the local students. One of them was Hala Abbas, the granddaughter of Mahmoud Abbas, the Palestinian president. They learned from Hala and her colleagues that if they wanted Palestinians to play the game, they had to refer to the Hamas organization as "militants" (instead of "terrorists," for example). As Asi and Tim learned more about the Palestinian side of the conflict, they realized their plan to leave the game without a concrete solution was untenable. They'd hoped to simply present the simulation and let people make up their own minds about the endgame. But it became clear that in order for Palestinians to embrace the game—or even want to play it in the first place—the game must embrace a two-state solution and an independent Palestinian state at the end of it.

The Israeli experience is very different. It's always been about the tension between the need for security and the need to gain the other side's trust. But for Palestinians, the desire seemed to be about having a strong leader who could face both his people and the larger world on the journey to statehood and sovereignty. Yasser Arafat was known for saying one thing in English and twisting the meaning completely when he spoke in Arabic. "The world expects the Palestinian leader to reject violence; but the Palestinians are proud of their resistance," Asi says. "Some see violence as necessary, as the only means of progress. What we learned from these students is that the most important factor for

Palestinians is having an independent state they can call their own."

Asi and Tim finally had enough information to flesh out the Palestinian side of the game and finish it. A few weeks after they returned from Qatar, Asi received an email message from a representative of Sheikha Mozah bint Nasser Al Missned, the second of the three wives of Sheikh Hamad bin Khalifa Al Thani, then emir of the State of Qatar. She was interested in what CMU in Qatar was up to, and the university selected three projects to show off, including PeaceMaker. The message Asi received read, "Her highness urges you to continue with this project."

As Asi and Tim got closer to finishing the game, the solution challenge kept cropping up. They decided to assume that the solution already existed: two independent states, Israel and Palestine, living in peace next to each other. However, the steps needed to build trust, to ensure security and freedom, and to get the necessary buy-in from both populations were taking much longer than expected. Leaders had tried their best in the past, some paying an incredible personal price—Egyptian president Anwar Sadat paid with his life for signing the agreement between Israel and Egypt, while Israeli prime minister Yitzhak Rabin was assassinated before reaching a final agreement with the Palestinians.

By this stage, another team member had joined Asi and Tim: Eric Brown, who was instrumental in developing local support for the game and helping Asi on the trip to Qatar. It was with Brown that Asi decided to co-found a video game company. "If we finished the game and confined its release to the academic circles, very few people would ever play it," Asi thought at the time. "It would become a museum item; people would say what a great job we'd done, and that would be it." Asi wanted to go big. Releasing the game commercially would mean that everyone could access it. He didn't want to be boxed in by the classroom. He wanted to create more PeaceMakers based on other conflicts—Iran and Korea, to begin with.

Everyone echoed that the game should be in schools and distributed by nonprofits. But Asi says he was naïve and stubborn. He thought people would line up around the block to buy this game. He and Eric sought legal advice and applied for some state funding. They got their first $100,000 through a state-funded grant program and used the connections they'd made over the years to draw more attention to the game. One early investor, a local and successful businessman named Bill Recker, was so impressed with the demo of the game that he pledged $300,000 on the spot. With the faculty's help, Asi and Eric also approached major game publishers, including EA and Microsoft. They all said the same thing: "Neat idea, but not marketable." Microsoft showed the most interest, but in the end muttered something about no one wanting to play a video game about politics. It was a sign of what was to come.

Using the money they'd raised, Asi and Eric rented an office on East Carson Street, the main street of South Side Pittsburgh, and called the company Impact Games. The shopfront was next to some very popular clubs, cafés, and sandwich shops; people constantly wandered in to ask what the hell they were selling. No one had heard of a video game company occupying a storefront on the street.

PeaceMaker launched on Amazon in 2007. After all of the

press it had already received and Asi, Ross, Eric, and Tim's efforts
to make it what it was, very few people bought it. It sold roughly
5,000 copies in the first couple of months. Asi was confused: He'd
received so many emails from all around the world—from the
UN, from world leaders. He'd printed all of them and stuck them
in a folder he kept on his desk. But now that the game was finally
out, where the hell were all those people who'd told him he'd done
a great job and encouraged him to keep going? Why wasn't the
UN buying so many copies of PeaceMaker that Asi and Eric could
barely keep up with demand?

It took them a while to realize that those people who'd written to them about PeaceMaker were not, in fact, representative of
the general public's interest in the game. They were more like the
only ones interested in the game.

That was a hard realization to come to. After the years of hard
work, the dream project was collapsing. Every morning, Asi and
Eric came to work and stared at the sales numbers on Amazon, hoping they'd gone up overnight. Every morning, they were disap-
pointed. Eventually, they understood how many factors had
escaped their attention. The game had come along too early, and
been too ambitious, to succeed commercially—this was before the
golden age of digital distribution. There was hardly any marketing
budget: they didn't think they'd need one, what with all the press
the game had already received.

Asi remembers telling Eric a few months before the release of
the game, "I don't want to see anything more than PeaceMaker in
a package on a store shelf. That's going to be enough for me." But
of course, it wasn't. Asi and the others had massively miscalculated,

with depressing results. PeaceMaker had gone overnight from a video game that could change the world to a very expensive art project.

Just as Asi was wondering what he was going to do with his life after spending three years making a game that nobody wanted to play, he received an email from his father, now a successful businessman. His father had followed PeaceMaker's progress and had an idea he wanted to run past Asi. "He'd warned me occasionally that the idea of PeaceMaker was bigger than the game itself. But the first time he played it, he loved it. Then he started raving to his friends about it," Asi says. "Look, you're not selling any copies of this, but it's too important to just forget about," Asi's father wrote. "Why don't we go to the Peres Center and convince them to do a wholesale deal?"

The Peres Center for Peace is an independent, nonpolitical organization founded by former Israeli president Shimon Peres in 1996, with the aim of working toward peace in the Middle East. The organization regularly holds conflict-resolution workshops and works with both Israelis and Palestinians to promote good relations. Here, finally, was Asi's chance to make a real contribution. If people at the heart of the Israeli-Palestinian conflict could play PeaceMaker and perhaps learn something about the conflict, and each other, wouldn't it all have been worthwhile?

Asi's father approached the center, whose representatives didn't need too much convincing. They offered to buy 100,000 copies of the game—80,000 copies to distribute for free through one of Israel's national newspapers and a Palestinian newspaper in the West Bank, and 20,000 copies to use in youth workshops.

And so, one morning in November 2008, Israelis and Palestinians alike opened their morning newspapers to find free copies of PeaceMaker. The stunt got a lot of public attention; once again, Asi was answering questions for national newspapers and Israeli radio. But the Peres Center workshops had the greatest impact. They still use PeaceMaker to this day.[6]

A few days after the game was distributed through Israeli newspapers, Asi and Eric got a call from a Disney executive named Leigh Zarelli. The company, which had a division for early acquisition, wanted to chat. Asi and Eric flew out to meet with Leigh, who took them to lunch at a flashy New York restaurant with a view of Central Park and offered them $10 million in cash for Impact Games.

"I wasn't sure what to say; of course, I was desperate to salvage the company and do something—anything—that would make all our efforts worthwhile," Asi says. "But Disney's idea wasn't exactly what I'd had in mind: they wanted a platform that could be used to turn any of Disney's brands and TV content into video games." That wasn't exactly the meaningful contribution Asi was hoping to make. But Asi and Eric were hopeful that under Disney's wing, they might be able to continue making video games about serious topics until, eventually, the world took notice.

Then came the global economic crisis of 2008. Asi and Eric's next meeting with Disney took place in Leigh's office at Disney HQ, on one of the worst days in the history of Wall Street. She barely listened to what they had to say; her eyes were glued to the television screen in her office. Disney dropped the offer. Asi could not blame the company for doing so, but the decision spelled the end for Impact Games. He left Impact; Eric kept the company and managed to sell it sometime later.

Asi went back to Israel for a while to clear his head. He visited the Peres Center to see what was being done with Peace-Maker. Even though the center was involved in youth education and hosted school workshops, it wasn't an officially sanctioned part of the Israeli education system; that would have been perceived as too sensitive or political. "I remember when I arrived someone telling me, only half joking, that they keep expecting the government to march in and shut the project down."

The PeaceMaker workshop Asi attended took place in the same Tel Aviv suburb in which he'd grown up. The attendees were well-educated, middle-class kids, all 17 and all Israelis. Asi sat at the back of this classroom. The instructor walked in and said, "Today, we're going to be playing a game." The kids looked around at each other, wide-eyed. Asi waited for the instructor to explain what PeaceMaker was all about and how to play it. Instead, she waved the kids over to the computers. "Right," she said. "Just start playing and we'll talk about it afterwards."

With no introduction to the game and no idea what they were about to experience, the kids jumped on the computers and started playing. Some seemed confused when the footage of the suicide bomb played on the screen; Asi heard one girl tell her friend excitedly, "Oh, so it's a war game!" Asi looked over their shoulders and was horrified. Most of them—if not all—had chosen to play as the Israeli PM. No surprises there. But they also seemed to miss the point of the game completely. One kid bombed the Palestinians over and over again.

"I'd never seen people playing the game this way. It's true, these kids didn't get the context before they jumped in, but the game is pretty self-explanatory. It's clear that it's about conflict resolution; it's not Call of Duty."

But these kids were doing something else, too: they were testing boundaries. They suddenly had the power that many of them had probably only fantasized about. "What would it be like if I were leading the country?" "What would I do?" It was, after all, a game. Asi now saw that PeaceMaker could just as soon be about playing out fantasies of power in a safe environment as it could be about building empathy. The students had taught him an important, albeit disturbing, lesson.

The instructor called a time-out. The kids got up from the computers and sat back down at their desks. She asked the kid who'd been repeatedly bombing the Palestinians, "Why did you do that?" The kid looked at her. "Because they're the enemy," he said flatly. The instructor asked him to elaborate. Over the course of the next hour, she asked each of them their thoughts on the Israeli-Palestinian conflict: What did they know? How did they feel about it?

Asi was amazed by the students' responses, but mostly by their general ignorance. The kids knew frighteningly little about the conflict, not grasping even the basics, such as why there was a conflict in the first place. The instructor put a map on the wall. "Can anyone tell me where Gaza is?" she asked. No one knew. They said Hamas was not connected to the Palestinian people. These kids weren't underprivileged—they all came from good schools. The public education system had let them down. The teachers didn't actually talk about the conflict in the classroom; it was seen as too sensitive a topic. And here, suddenly, was a game that let students do whatever they wanted—pick sides and then talk openly about the conflict.

Asi found the process alarming to watch. The following year, most of these kids were going to be in the army, making very real and very important decisions. How could they be expected to make the right choices when they didn't even know the basic facts about what was going on? Asi was glad that PeaceMaker had helped in some small way. But he also realized that he'd been so preoccupied with changing people's minds about the situation that he'd missed this other possible function of the game: simply teaching facts about the conflict and its context. How can someone feel empathy for another's opinions if they don't even know what those opinions are in the first place?

Asi came to understand that the game itself had perhaps been a little premature. "Imagine making a game like that today, when the world is a lot more receptive to new technology that helps them see the world differently. I'm not just talking about a better-looking game that has fancy graphics and more immersive scenarios, but about awareness, connectivity—the increasing power of social media."

People continue to refer to PeaceMaker after all these years. There's continued media interest, especially when the Israeli-Palestine conflict is back in the headlines. But Asi also continues to hear from people who still play the game, or discover it for the first time. For him, this proves that not only is the game still relevant, but also that the idea of a video game teaching someone about a complex situation, and fostering in that person a sense of empathy, is more accepted now than it was in 2007.

When Asi returned to the United States, he got a call from

an organization called Games for Change. That nonprofit became the umbrella organization for games with a purpose, games that have goals beyond entertainment alone. "They asked me to help them grow, and I said yes." Asi ended up leading the organization as an executive director from 2010 to 2015.

Asi is often asked how things have changed since the early days of PeaceMaker. Although the game did not do well commercially, its impact has been undeniable. Not only did it prove that games could be much more than entertainment, but it helped unify all the other games and game developers in this field under the banner of games for change. It inspired a new movement that has since become a significant area of the video game industry.

Eisenberg, the pioneering teacher from CMU, and Dr. Cleotilde Gonzalez, a research professor in social and decision sciences, went on to use PeaceMaker to better understand decision making in conflict resolution. Dr. Gonzalez later published several papers on the game, including one in the journal *Computers in Human Behavior*,[7] which used data collected in Israel when the game was tested on students there.

"We saw that young Israelis were far more willing to explore the different possible actions when playing the Palestinian than the Israeli side," Gonzalez said recently. "This means Israeli students were less willing to explore new scenarios in their own role, and thus less successful in resolving the conflict from that perspective. Again, putting people in others' shoes helps."

She also studied the effects of repeated playing. "The most meaningful finding was that with repeated plays of the game, the relationships between the person's political assumptions and value system they hold to before playing, and the performance in the game, decreased. This means that they did better over time, from one session to the next, and it often meant taking action that is misaligned [with] or even contradicts their original beliefs. So it is possible to put someone in the other side's shoes and reduce the effect of personal bias while engaging in conflict-resolution exercises."

Now, imagine how powerful games like PeaceMaker can be in bringing about cultural understanding and speaking directly to younger generations in their preferred language.

This is just the beginning.

2.

A Former Supreme Court Judge Takes Matters into Her Own Hands

(THE STORY OF ICIVICS)

n July 2010, former Supreme Court justice Sandra Day O'Connor took the podium at the Games for Change conference in New York.[1] Wearing a smart, mint-green tailored jacket and her trademark white coif, O'Connor quipped: "I had to ask myself, 'What am I doing at Games for Change?' I'm an old grandmother, I'm not a techie!" The crowd cheered.

O'Connor was there to promote a new interactive civics curriculum that would, she hoped, help fill the gaping hole in the American public's knowledge of how the branches of government actually work—particularly the role of judges and the court system. "If someone had told me when I retired from the Supreme Court about a couple of years ago that I would be speaking at a conference about digital games, I would have been very skeptical, maybe thinking you had one drink too many," she told a packed auditorium[2] at Parsons School of Design. She went on, "Let's face it. Civics can be pretty boring. There used to be an 800-page textbook—you could hardly pick it up without injuring your back."

Over the years, O'Connor had often noted how frequently judges came under fire when something went wrong with a highly publicized case. A former law clerk of O'Connor's, Kathleen Smalley, stopped by O'Connor's chambers on a visit to Washington some years after her clerkship. "There was a set of abortion cases before the court that term, and they were highly publicized," Smalley told us recently. "They were literally moving boxes full of mail to the justice about them. I asked her which way the sentiment was running. She wouldn't tell me, but she did say the [writers of the letters] were absolutely consistent in threatening that, if she didn't rule the way they thought she should, they would never vote for her again."

The thing is, you can't vote for Supreme Court justices—they're appointed by the president and serve for life. "All these people who were writing in were sure they knew what the constitution provides on abortion—but they actually knew so little about our system of government that they didn't realize that we don't vote for justices."

O'Connor herself was nominated to the Supreme Court by Ronald Reagan in 1981; she won unanimous approval from the Senate and became the first female justice to be appointed to the court, serving until her retirement, in 2006. Born in El Paso, Texas, in 1930, O'Connor graduated from Stanford University's law school in 1952 before taking a job at the county attorney's office in San Mateo, California.[3] After serving as a civilian lawyer in Germany, she returned to the United States to work in private practice before being appointed one of Arizona's assistant attorneys general. When the state senator from her district resigned in 1969, then-governor Jack Williams appointed O'Connor to replace him. In 1972, she was appointed as the Republican majority leader in the state Senate before joining the Supreme Court.

Even though O'Connor is a Republican, she wasn't always conservative in her decision making. She frequently advocated for women's rights and opposed the Republican call, in the 1992 case *Planned Parenthood v. Casey*, to overturn the landmark abortion rights decision, *Roe v. Wade.*

After retiring from the bench in 2006, O'Connor's attention turned to American's woeful understanding of civics. "[Young voters] lack confidence in their ability to discuss specific issues like the economy, health care, or foreign affairs," O'Connor, now 86, told us recently. "Clearly, something is wrong."

At first, O'Connor concentrated simply on the state of the judiciary, founding the Sandra Day O'Connor Project on the State of the Judiciary at Georgetown Law Center, where she convened a conference, along with Justice Stephen G. Breyer, on the topic. O'Connor was worried that the independence of the judiciary was being compromised by the amount of money being poured into judicial elections by political forces and by the increasing threats to impeach judges for unpopular decisions.

Her aim was to come up with solutions, but she didn't want the conference to be aimed entirely at academics. So she invited educators, policymakers, and Warren Buffett.

"One of the takeaways from this was that people . . . just didn't know what judges do," says Julie O'Sullivan, who clerked for

O'Connor in the Supreme Court after graduating from Cornell Law School. Education seemed the obvious answer—and the earlier, the better.

At first, O'Connor conceived of the project as a Civics 101–style book, but she soon realized that that wasn't necessarily an improvement on the stale, outdated textbooks that students were already being subjected to. The goal was to create something that kids would actually get excited about.

O'Sullivan wondered if an interactive book would be better. She asked O'Connor for her opinion and was met with a blank stare. O'Connor didn't know much about the internet. "When we showed her a hyperlink, she was like, 'Oh Julie, that's so clever!'"

O'Connor and O'Sullivan partnered with Georgetown and Arizona State University (ASU), where O'Connor had connections who were, as O'Sullivan puts it, "good at tech stuff." One weekend, O'Connor and O'Sullivan assembled a group of award-winning civics teachers, from all over the country, who in the past had expressed interest in using tech to revitalize the civics curriculum. They congregated at Georgetown to spitball ideas of what an interactive civics project for middle school kids might look like. The teachers worked in teams over the weekend to come up with proposals and met on Sunday afternoon in a stuffy lecture hall to present their ideas.

One teacher suggested the virtual world of Second Life, in which users create figures, representing themselves, that interact with other users' avatars. The teacher had used Second Life to make an avatar of O'Connor, which she showed the group. O'Connor was immediately taken with it—at least until someone else in the group pointed out the difficulty of conducting any kind of strict civics curriculum amid the general lawlessness of the avatars.

But there was something about the idea of using digital tools that appealed to O'Sullivan. The next day, she called her brother, then the head of the Interactive Telecommunications Program at Tisch School of the Arts at New York University (NYU). She told him about the events of the weekend and asked if he had any good ideas for where she should look next. "What about Games for Change?" he suggested.

The organization, founded in 2004, was gaining traction with its annual festival, an event promoting video games focused on social issues. What about a video game? O'Sullivan thought. "So I called [O'Connor] up and said, 'Look, why don't you do this?' And she told me, 'Great. Why don't *you* do it?' And I was like, 'No way, I know nothing about technology,' and she said, 'That's okay, you'll learn.'"

At first, O'Sullivan laughed off the suggestion, which was typical of O'Connor. "She does not believe in accepting barriers," she told us. "Maybe it is the pioneer mentality." In any case, O'Sullivan pursued the idea because she felt she owed O'Connor; the justice's decision to hire her had changed O'Sullivan's life. Plus, O'Connor had been a good friend through the years, and O'Sullivan felt that it was only right to do this for her old boss if she could. "Believe me, it was not career-enhancing. It was more like, career-distracting. Nor did I have any natural interest in the project—it was just meant to be an interesting suggestion, for crying out loud!"

The initial idea was for a six-month project, but as O'Sullivan and O'Connor talked to teachers, administrators, and educational organizations about the state of the country's civics curriculum, it became obvious that more than a temporary fix was needed. The project would have to revolutionize the way civics is taught in the United States, starting with middle school.

Although it was O'Sullivan's brother who initially pointed her in the direction of video games, he was soon trying to talk his sister out of the idea: successful games, he told her, cost tens of millions of dollars, and they are not made overnight. "But then we said to ourselves, hang on a minute, we're not exactly competing with World of Warcraft here, are we?" O'Sullivan thought. "All we need to do is make a game, or a series of games, which are more compelling than what's currently going on in civics classrooms. Which, let's face it, is not hard." (In reaching this viewpoint, O'Sullivan may have been helped by her son, who was seven years old at the time—or, at least, by the expression on his face after she asked him what he did in his civics lessons.)

The real turning point occurred during a board meeting at ASU among O'Sullivan, O'Connor, and a few of O'Connor's other former clerks. The board also invited Dr. James Gee, a celebrated sociolinguist and pioneer in the field of new literacy. Gee had moved to ASU after publishing the book *What Video Games Have to Teach Us about Learning and Literacy*. The book argued that games, when made and played the right way, can motivate and challenge players, and that teachers and educators could apply the same methodology in classrooms.[4] A lot of games are about problem solving. Most curriculums focus on facts, which are difficult to retain by rote learning without some real-world scenario to attach them to. Games use facts as tools for problem solving; a person's simple act of utilizing a piece of information to solve a particular puzzle means that the information is much more likely to stick in his or her brain.

Gee's thesis was groundbreaking: he didn't just speak of using games as learning tools, but suggested modeling an entire education system on them. Later, Gee's book would serve, in part, as the blueprint for video game initiatives at the Gates and MacArthur Foundations and for projects including the Quest to Learn school in Manhattan (which we cover in Chapter 9), where the curriculum is based on gaming principles and outcomes.

Gee got the idea of studying games by watching his six-year-old son playing Pajama Sam, a problem-solving game. When Gee saw how amused and enthralled his son was, he began playing games himself to figure out what makes a good one so compelling. He got his hands on whatever he could find: kids' games, puzzle games, platformers, first-person shooters, and role-playing games.

When Gee arrived at ASU, the MacArthur Foundation approached him about investigating a small project launched by O'Connor. Part of the mission of the foundation's Digital Media & Learning initiative, launched in 2006, was to explore the potential of digital media in changing the way young people learn and communicate. "They told me to check it out, to see if it was viable," Gee recalled recently. Gee found two teams at ASU, as well as people from Georgetown University, working on the project separately. "The two teams were each competing for control of the project with different ideas about how to proceed," Gee said. "This had led to [O'Connor] and her closest colleagues having concerns." Gee told the MacArthur Foundation that the project would not be ready for prime time, so to speak, unless someone integrated the teams and better focused the project. The foundation asked him to do it and report back on whether the project seemed viable.

So Gee set up a meeting at the ASU Law School (which is actually named after O'Connor: the Sandra Day O'Connor College of Law) with the former justice and her closest colleagues on the project. When Gee got to the meeting, there was clearly tension in the room surrounding ASU's involvement with the project, though O'Connor, who had never met Gee, came up to him, introduced herself, and offered to get him a cup of coffee.

The first thing Gee did was to tell O'Connor that he was going to use the MacArthur money to change and integrate the teams, so that they could work together with a shared vision. "The second thing I had to do was deal with the issue of games," Gee said. From the outset, O'Connor's vision had been to reach young people through digital media. While she did not know a lot about digital media, she knew that young people were attracted to it. "Some of the team members had been pushing video games as the favored form of digital media, but the justice had quite negative reactions about the word 'game,'" Gee said. "She is a woman with strong opinions—opinions which she can articulate clearly and defend strongly. But she is also a woman who truly listens, understands, and will change her mind if she is convinced."

Gee explained that the common view of video games—all violence and shooting—was wrong. He pointed to one of the best-selling games in history, The Sims, a life-simulation game in which players look after virtual characters called Sims, doing everything from caring for their well-being to making decisions about what kind of jobs they have and whom they marry. Gee pointed out The Sims is not a violent game and that the majority of its players are girls and women.

More importantly, Gee explained to O'Connor that games are simply well-designed problem-solving spaces where gamers are taught, through the games' design, to persist past failure and gain mastery. He added that even though school treats fields like physics and civics as sets of facts or bodies of information, in reality, they are sets of activities, problems, problem-solving tools. "Civics should be seen as much about how one becomes a proactive participant in society as it is about facts and information," Gee told O'Connor. Therefore, games could allow teachers to set students up as problem solvers in civics, and not just memorizers of inert facts. Finally, Gee mentioned that, in his view, society had become quite poor at working collaboratively to solve problems, in part thanks to its political divisions and the diminished feelings of "co-citizenship" on the part of many Americans. "I told [O'Connor] that I was not an advocate for bringing games to school all by themselves, but only as an integral part of a wider curriculum with good texts, activities and tools for interaction and participation in the real world."

O'Connor seemed convinced. "He was able to convey, with such ease and eloquence, the power of video games on learning," she told us. It was Gee who facilitated O'Connor's keynote appearance at the Games for Change festival in New York shortly after the meeting. "She came early and listened to other people's presentations about games that dealt with all sorts of important national and global issues." After the talk, Gee was in an elevator with O'Connor when someone nudged O'Connor on the shoulder and mentioned hearing that she did not like the word "game."

"She said—in her inimitable way—'No, that's the word they use and I'm fine with it.'" O'Connor has since become a convert. "I have seen my own grandchildren maneuver the computer, and they are quick and completely engaged in what they are doing," she says. "The medium of video games allows for concepts—which admittedly can be hard to grasp in civics—to happen to us. Essentially, this spirals down to a simple principle: you learn best by doing."

The MacArthur Foundation agreed to fund the project, which O'Connor and O'Sullivan named iCivics, in order to emphasize all of the branches of government. Realizing that the project would require a separate staff, organization, and funding arm to run, O'Connor split from Georgetown University and, later, from ASU. O'Sullivan called up old friends and acquaintances to ask for volunteers. "People used to tease us and call us 'bumblebees'— because it was impossible for us to fly," O'Sullivan said. "We had two people, and no money."

Smalley, O'Connor's former law clerk, who had remained friends with the justice, soon became concerned that O'Connor was taking on too much work. She was, after all, supposed to be retired. "When I spoke to her about this, she had been retired for ten months, and hadn't played golf even once," Smalley says. Smalley led a fund-raising effort to create a fellowship and hired a young lawyer, Abigail Taylor, to help O'Connor and O'Sullivan with the launch of iCivics. (Smalley later joined the board when it became an independent organization. "Once a law clerk, always a law clerk," she says. "If the justice asks you to do something, you get to work.")

Taylor, a Harvard Law graduate with expressive brown eyes,

knew something about games and education. Her mother, a television producer, had been responsible for putting together the successful children's television adaptation of the video game *Where in the World Is Carmen Sandiego?* (The show aired on PBS from 1991 to 1995 and came about partly as a response to a National Geographic Society report on geographic literary in the United States,[5] which found that one in four adults could not locate the Pacific Ocean on a world map.) Not only did Taylor play the video game growing up, but once her mother began working on the show, Taylor became a kind of guinea pig—reading scripts, listening to pitches in the car, and tolerating a constant stream of questions about what parts of the game she liked and didn't like. As a reward, she got to watch the pilot being filmed.

Now that Gee had persuaded O'Connor and her team to pursue a gaming project, the next step was figuring out whether the project would focus on kids inside the classroom or outside it. O'Connor and the others decided that it would be too hard to reach kids outside the classroom, when there would be so many other things competing for their attention. So the project took the form of a website with a number of interactive games that civics teachers could access whenever they wanted. That decision was an important and smart one; rather than one game, a portfolio of smaller games would mitigate risk and allow more ideas and directions to be explored.

The principals then considered the games themselves. What would they look like? Early concepts were ambitious. "We wanted a big, immersive civic world—games that could take days or months or years to play—you know, like World of Warcraft," Taylor told us recently. She was Skyping in from Boston, where she now lives with her partner, Jeff Curley, and their one-year-old son, Jack. Taylor and Curley started dating while working at iCivics. The two had been friends in college, and when Taylor joined the project, she realized that she and her colleagues needed someone to handle public relations and marketing. At the time, Curley was working in e-commerce and digital marketing for Marriott Hotels. Taylor called Curley and asked if he'd be interested in joining this somewhat vague, understaffed project involving education and civic learning. For the next four years, Taylor and Curley became close colleagues and friends. They spent countless hours together, at all hours of the day and night. "It was stressful and hectic but so exciting, and we did all of it together," Taylor said. After Taylor left iCivics, she and Curley both missed the intensity of their working relationship. "And that's when we realized we wanted to be together in life, if not in work." For Taylor, it was a natural, if at times confusing, transition, and within a few months Curley had moved out of his place and into hers. "The hardest part, to be honest, was explaining all of this to people who had known us only as colleagues." The couple's son, Jack, is now known as "the iCivics baby."

When O'Sullivan hired Curley, he was put in charge of the distribution plan for iCivics—mostly figuring out how to get the games in front of teachers. Early efforts mainly involved using O'Connor to raise the profile of the project; she even went on *The Daily Show with Jon Stewart,*[6] which both Taylor and Curley thought was hilarious, since O'Connor had never seen the program. O'Connor, wearing a light blue sweater and black and gold earrings, held her own against Stewart, matching him quip for quip. She told Stewart that Americans are more likely to know the names of the *American Idol* judges than the branches of government, and finished, "How do you like that?" Stewart loved it. "We're going to need more than a website," he told her.

The strategy worked. Smalley praised O'Connor's efforts in spreading the word about iCivics. "The nightly comedy news shows, for instance, are not her natural milieu, but she took advantage of every effective forum to get the message out that our country desperately needs an educated and engaged citizenry, and we have been too lax for too long in educating students about our political system and their role in it," she said. "She was able to bring other judges and political figures to the cause, and her star power drew great support."

EVERYONE WHO HEARD ABOUT O'Connor's mission agreed that it was sorely needed and long overdue. While civic learning had once formed the foundation of the educational curriculum in the United States, it was now in the midst of a decades-long decline. The most popular piece of evidence in support of this at the time was a national survey conducted by the National Constitution Center and released at a US Senate hearing in September 1998,[7] a week prior to the 211th anniversary of the signing of the US Constitution. The survey compared teens' knowledge of pop culture with their knowledge of the Constitution, with farcical results: more could name the star of *The Fresh Prince of Bel-Air* than were able to name the chief justice of the US Supreme Court (94.7 percent versus 2.2 percent); more knew which city has the zip code "90210" than knew the city in which the US Constitution was written (75 percent versus 25 percent); and more were able to confidently and accurately name the stars of the film *Titanic* than were able to identify the vice president of the United States at the time (90 percent versus 74 percent).

Until the 1960s, civics courses in American high schools focused on three things: respectively, the role of citizens, current issues and events, and the structure and function of the government at the national level.[8] But as the national focus on education shifted gradually toward science, technology, engineering, and mathematics (STEM), civics struggled to keep up. The 2006 National Assessment of Education Progress (NAEP), a Department of Education–administered test for more than 25,000 fourth-, eighth-, and twelfth-graders, showed that no group demonstrated a significant increase in performance[9] since the previous NAEP test, in 1998. Only 75 percent of fourth-graders knew that only citizens can vote in the United States. "The absence of civic content from assessments signals its status as a second-class subject, a conclusion held by too many superintendents, principals, teachers, and students nationwide," the campaign concluded in its 2011 report.

The Campaign for the Civic Mission Schools report also pointed to some staggering findings about Americans' involvement in civic life: according to answers from the Annenberg Public Policy Center surveys in the decade before the report's publication, only one-third of Americans could name all three branches of government (which O'Connor mentioned in her Games for Change Festival speech in 2010) while almost a third believed, wrongly, that a US Supreme Court ruling could be appealed. (One of the most disturbing findings in the report was about President Barack Obama: according to the report, a year into his term, 32 percent of Americans still believed he was a Muslim, while 25 percent thought he was born outside the United States.)

The report also alluded to the low levels of civic engagement, a concern often voiced by O'Connor herself: despite the 2008 presidential election having generated the highest voter turnout in over 40 years, only 56.8 percent of eligible voters actually voted, meaning that nearly half of the American population eligible to vote—roughly one hundred million people—did not.

SHORTLY AFTER THE ASU presentation, Gee put Taylor in touch with Filament Games, then a three-person game studio based in Wisconsin. Dan Norton, Filament's chief creative officer, co-founded the company after seeing an opportunity to make learning games "that don't suck." Gee gave Norton and his co-founder, Dan White, a helping hand; White had been Gee's student at the University of Wisconsin, where Gee had helped start the Games, Learning and Society Center with six other faculty members, with the aim of investigating video games' potential for learning and designing games for this purpose.

Filament Games grew out of the project; Gee even gave White school credit while he and Norton worked on their first games. "Their success was rooted in the fact that they had a deep allegiance to game design," Gee said. "We saw a lot of great research and rhetoric being crafted about the possibilities of learning games, but not a lot of people actually attempting to make those things," he told us recently.

Norton remembers Gee's eagerness to make the partnership

work. "I distinctly remember Jim telling us that if we blew it on this project, he'd be forced to murder us." Happily, that was not the case. iCivics launched in February 2009 with two games. The first, Do I Have a Right, in which players run their own law firm and answer clients' questions about the Bill of Rights, is still the number one–played title on iCivics. In the game, players take on the role of a lawyer in charge of a constitutional law firm. Potential clients come in, requesting help with their problems and asking whether or not they have rights in given situations. Sometimes, the problems presented are downright silly, as with the client who wants to trap his brother in the basement. But more often than not, clients' problems are tied to specific rights acknowledged in the US Constitution. The player must ascertain what the rights are and send that information to a lawyer in the firm who can help the client with a specific problem. Along the way, players can hire new lawyers, upgrade their firm, and learn more about the core constitutional rights. Curley: "I remember when we were early talking about it, we were loosely basing it off Diner Dash. It gets stressful the more you play. You hire more lawyers, clients coming in thick and fast, decisions get more complex. The kids who are really into it, they love it because it takes some time to master."

Social studies teachers had been so starved for new and interesting public resources that they responded enthusiastically: iCivics received 50,000 unique users in the first year. Taylor and Curley would frequently travel to teaching and educational technology conferences around the country, speaking to teachers and showing them the site.

Soon enough, word of mouth took over. O'Connor, O'Sullivan,

Taylor, and Curley began receiving letters of thanks from civics teachers around the country. But the feedback was always the same: "This is great, but we need more." As iCivics slowly acquired new partners and funding, the team put their heads together to identify new topics and learning objectives that could be transformed into games and, after that, a curriculum. There was a lot of trial and error. "The struggles were to be expected— it's hard to make a game, and it's even harder to make a successful game that teaches," Norton said. "We had to put a lot of effort into length of playtime to make sure games could work in classrooms, and some of the games were very tricky to pull off in terms of performance in Flash on older machines."

In May 2010, iCivics launched a revamped website with games like Branches of Power, which aims to help students understand the function of each government branch, and Win the White House, about the presidential electoral process. The games place students in different civic roles to give them agency to address real-world problems. For example, in a game called Executive Command, players take on the role of POTUS (president of the United States). They are required to pick a presidential agenda (such as health or education), sign and veto bills, and work with those in the administration to enact laws. They are also responsible for leading the United States military during war.

The gameplay varies widely from one game to another, based on the learning objectives. In some games, including Executive Command, the focus is on fixing the player with an identity that has both goals and constraints. Unlike a book or television documentary about the role of a country's president, a game gives players the chance to actually *act*, make decisions similar to those of a president, and thus create an experience. In that regard, this way of learning is unmatched by any passive medium. "Facts are important, but students must also learn how to use them," O'Connor told us.

Each game took between two and four months to make. O'Sullivan's son, Danny, interned with iCivics when he was a freshman in college; his job was to go around to public schools in DC to test the games with kids in the classroom. Often, there would be pleas for him to come back the next day. "A lot of kids would ask him if they could play the games at home, in their own time," O'Sullivan said. Even O'Connor play-tested the games, albeit with the help of Danny and her nephews. The young men warmed O'Connor up by having her play the popular video game Civilization, a process O'Sullivan remembers as "hysterical": "[O'Connor] would say, 'Let's go build a courthouse, now!' She became so enamored with the technology, convinced of how vital it was."

iCivics also launched a fully integrated civics curriculum, developed by a former teacher named Alison Atwater. Atwater joined iCivics around the same time as Taylor, in late 2007. After spending eight years teaching in a middle school in Arizona, Atwater began law school at ASU, where one of her professors, Charles Calleros, had agreed to help O'Sullivan and O'Connor write some teaching materials that would be integrated into the project when it launched. When Calleros learned that Atwater had once been a teacher, he enlisted her help. "I remember I had a civics textbook I taught from—it was run of the mill, nothing special," she told us over Skype recently. "I would jazz it up by embellishing as we read, trying to get the kids interested by telling stories. It was hard to find any online resources back then. At the school where I taught, we had a computer lab that we were expected to use, but it wasn't easy to figure out what to actually do in there."

Atwater began helping Calleros with the curriculum materials, writing lesson plans in a fun, conversational tone that would be easy for middle-schoolers to understand. When Filament Games began working on the first game, Atwater was hired to write content for the game, including dialogue. After graduating, in 2010, Atwater interned with the chief justice of the Arizona Supreme Court. Meanwhile, she kept writing lesson plans for iCivics. "I was mainly thinking about what I wish I had when I was teaching, and using that as inspiration," Atwater said of her lesson plans. These included both sections of text ("fun, conversational, and chatty") and activities ("engaging, and yet easy for teachers to grade"). In a lesson plan about the executive branch, titled A Very Big Branch, among the different lesson activities, students distinguish real-life examples of enforcement activities from examples of work related to regulations, in order to learn the difference between those two executive branch functions. In another example, given a list of hypothetical statements cabinet members might make to the president, students identify which department of the executive branch each speaker leads.

BY 2012, CURLEY WAS the deputy director of iCivics—both O'Sullivan and Taylor had left, O'Sullivan to resume teaching and Taylor to pursue a career in law. Around the same time, Louise

Dube, a trained lawyer from Boston with an MBA from Yale, was arguing with her son, Daniel, then in fourth grade. Daniel had come home from school one day and told his mother he needed to go play a video game. She responded that after school was not the time for video games, and that he would have to do homework instead. "No mom, this *is* homework," Daniel corrected her. Mrs. Brown, Daniel's teacher, had assigned her students to play Win the White House, an iCivics game, to learn about the electoral system. The national election was just around the corner. "Really?" Dube said, raising an eyebrow. "Really," Daniel replied. After Daniel played the game, he turned to Dube. "Mom, all of school should be like iCivics."

Daniel was a born reformer. He had multiple theories about how to run a school system, which he often shared, perhaps too liberally, with his teachers. But that day, Dube took notice. "I knew iCivics was different," she told us recently. "I had worked for over 20 years in educational technology, asking my kids to click through multiple-choice questions only to be met with: 'Do I have to do this again?'" After Daniel played the game, he asked Dube about the elected representatives for their district. Fortunately, Dube knew the answers. "He even urged me to vote in the local election—not once, but every year since then."

Dube grew up in Quebec City, Canada. She studied law at McGill University in Montreal before going to Yale. Dube's mother was the second female justice on the Canadian Supreme Court—the "Ruth Bader Ginsburg of Canada," as she puts it. (Ginsburg was the second female justice on the US Supreme Court after O'Connor; she was appointed by Bill Clinton in 1993.)

Dube's mother shared a lot of the same experiences, and frustrations, that O'Connor faced. Neither woman could, for example, get a job out of law school—O'Connor had to take an unpaid position, while Dube's mother put an ad in the newspaper to find work. "From that vantage point, I saw firsthand the sacrifices that women of that generation made to make our careers possible," Dube said.

After business school, Dube co-founded an alternative-to-incarceration program in New York called Cases, which advocates for the release of youthful felony offenders to caseworkers in order to reduce incarceration costs and improve long-term outcomes. One of the services first offered by Cases was a manual skills training program. "To improve opportunities, we decided to develop an option for academic skill development, and created a school," Dube said. Dube and her team developed a curriculum designed around the experience of living in New York, using the city as a contextual device for learning. This meant moving away from a construction skills–based approach and toward a general education program. "We decided that making learning relevant was the best approach, and while gaming was not part of our plan, we had a math curriculum that included references to the Manhattan road grid, and proportions using New York everyday life situations," Dube said.

Then, in 2013, she met Curley at SXSWedu, the South by Southwest festival's education conference. At the purely social event they both attended, the two got along. Curley told Dube that iCivics was looking for a new executive director, but the position was in DC, and Dube didn't want to move. Later on,

Curley contacted Dube to discuss opening an iCivics office in Boston. "I remembered my experience with Daniel—the number one iCivics fan—and decided to take the position."

Dube assumed leadership in 2014. Things went well: revenues in the 2013 financial year had been $1.7 million; in 2015, this number increased to $1.9 million, plus $317,000 in endowment raised, for a total of $2.2 million. "I would say that at that stage, they had accomplished what the organization set out to do—prove that civics education could be engaging," Dube said. "But not yet accomplished its mission to reimagine civics education and make civics education ubiquitous."

One of Dube's first tasks was to gather more resources, partnerships, and a bigger team to accomplish the second goal. That would mean changing the project's fund-raising model, recruiting more staff (there are currently 11 team members, in both DC and Boston), and raising iCivics' visibility.

iCivics now reaches three million students across the United States every year. According to a number of evaluation studies conducted by iCivics in partnerships with universities and third-party groups, looking at everything from the games' impact in classrooms to the acquisition of civic knowledge, some 100,000 teachers are registered and use iCivics, and 50 percent of middle school social studies teachers use the program, in all 50 states. That means that today, iCivics reaches half of all middle-schoolers in the country.[10]

The program continues to grow at the rate of 2,000 to 3,000 new teachers per month during the school year. There are now 19 games, 2 digital tools, and 120 lesson plans on the site. One study showed that the proportion of kids who play the games unprompted at home after being introduced to them in school is now 45 percent—almost one in two.

In 2009, the Persephone Group, an educational evaluation service, conducted an independent assessment of iCivics' effectiveness[11] by studying students in sixth, seventh, and eighth grades in 22 classrooms across 13 states. Each student was given a test before and a test after playing the iCivics game, Do I Have a Right.

The study also included observations of students who received iCivics lesson plans and played the games, as well as teacher surveys and feedback. The results showed that student test scores improved by 13.7 percent after students played Do I Have a Right once. The scores of those students who played at least twice improved by 18.3 percent; and after playing the game in class, 57 percent of students played Do I Have a Right in their free time at home, unprompted. "We know from independent research that iCivics does work," O'Connor told us. "It increases civic knowledge, helps people become better writers, and even inspires people to get involved in their communities. My vision is set on shaping the next generations for informed and honest participation in our democracy."

Anecdotally, things look even more promising. In 2014, iCivics conducted an eight-week pilot project in Indianapolis, in which it partnered with a library in a low-income district. Participants in the project played iCivics games. According to Dube, a 29-year-old man with limited reading skills came in every day to play his favorite two games: Responsibility Launcher and Cast Your Vote. In Responsibility Launcher, the player is Liberty Belle, a magical fairy who may or may not be the pixie reincarnation of George Washington. The player's job is to fire anvils of "civic duty" at citizens who don't understand how to fulfill their obligations as civically active Americans. ("Match the right anvil with the right problem to minimize headaches!") In Cast Your Vote, players get to ask the questions in a debate between two candidates running for a government office. Players rate the quality of the answers and choose which answers they agree with. Ultimately, players must cast their votes based on the answers of the candidates. (The similarities to real life are intentional.)

Dube continues to get emails from teachers and users of iCivics. One teacher wrote in to say that she'd tried an iCivics game with her ninth-grade civics students after they'd learned about the Bill of Rights. While her first-period class is usually quiet and a little difficult to engage (its morning, and they're tired), she found that they perked up considerably when they realized they'd be playing a game for the whole class period. One student even shouted, "This is fun, AND I'm learning!" Another time, a student wrote in to say that he'd played a number of iCivics games as homework, and his takeaway was the realization that it's actually really hard to be a politician.

Taylor says that iCivics not only serves a pedagogical need; it's also the most fun homework middle-schoolers are assigned. The curriculum is now so easy to use that teachers can pull a whole Standards Aligned System unit from the iCivics site: lesson plans, games, etc. The whole system has been designed to be accessible, and easy to use, for both teachers and students. "If you just need a game for the kids to play on a Friday, and you have the computer lab, you stick them in front of Do I Have a Right and it still works," Taylor says.

There was a fair amount of skepticism to begin with—both

Taylor and Curley acknowledge this. "Social studies teachers had been feeling left out in the cold for a long time," Curley said. He gave the following example: if you Google "middle school science curriculum," you get 100 million hits. But if you Google "middle school civics curriculum," you maybe get 500,000. Smalley's sister, a fourth-grade teacher, recently called to ask Smalley to give a talk about the three branches of government in front of her class. "Suddenly, one of her students gave me a very stern look as I summarized the three branches, and pointed out that the most important thing was the trunk of the tree: the people," Smalley said. "[O'Connor] loved that story, and she sent signed books to the whole class."

Now that many middle-schoolers are confident enough in their civics knowledge to correct a former law clerk, the next challenge for Dube and iCivics is tackling high schools. "The short-term goal is to expand the curriculum upwards and make sure it's more complex and challenging," Curley says. This means creating more graphically mature games that appeal to older students and modernizing the tech by moving into mobile and cross-platform spaces. "Long term, I'd love to see [iCivics] become a textbook replacement for classrooms. Could you just put away your Pearson and McGraw-Hill textbooks and just take a semester of iCivics?"

Dube also wants more assessment of the educational value of games—whether they offer an adequate investment-to-learning trade-off, or truly reimagine the learning process, or simply glam up traditional learning mechanics. "Games will form part of an ecosystem, an increasingly important one that will help students experience learning as relevant," she said. "At the end of this process of change, I would hope that education is a different experience than what I or my kids experienced, where 'going to school' is a positive active experience that students can customize [and] learning becomes something you would want to do your whole life."

Norton agrees. "I'm not looking or hoping for children floating in VR [virtual reality] immersion tanks with their curriculum being pumped into their spinal cord plugs. My hope is that more great learning games get into more classrooms, and that we can create moments of agency, reflection, and empowerment that get people excited and passionate about learning a thing they didn't know, sharing it and using it."

For the time being, iCivics is focused on product development: overseeing game upgrades, writing new lesson plans, and resolving issues and updating content on the website. (iCivics' largest traffic day was on Constitution Day in 2015; the site received over one million unique page views.) There's also a focus on fundraising, planning events, writing grants, supporting teachers, and marketing daily through social media.

O'Connor continues to be involved, albeit remotely. Her ambitions for the project have grown. "I wanted to change the status quo," she told us. "I wanted to alter not only how civics was taught, but our goals for civics education. We need our youth to feel engaged. We need young people to be conscious that they too can have real impact."

"[O'Connor] says the two people she met in her life that were truly great were Nelson Mandela and Eleanor Roosevelt—they both had magnetic energy that inspired others to do things," Taylor said. "She's the only person I've met who has that."

"I have often said that iCivics is the most important thing I have ever done," O'Connor continued. "More so even than serving 25 years on the highest court in this nation. What is needed most is for local, state, and federal policymakers to recognize that preparing students for informed and engaged citizenship is just as important as preparing students for college and a career. In fact, they go hand in hand. Civics fuels students' curiosity for the world around them. Civics encourages them to become cultured and discriminating individuals. My goal for iCivics is to see more students get involved with their communities, vote, and be productive, engaged members of society. As a former state senator, yes, I would love to see more young people run for office and wrestle with political issues, but not everyone will have the capacity or interest to do that. At the very least, I hope that iCivics will make a significant contribution to a better dialogue and ensure a vibrant and robust future for our democracy."

"We've seen a number of generations pass through the school system without an understanding of our government," Curley told us before he and Taylor took their son, Jack, off to bed. "This hurts the folks who have the least access to power. iCivics is a way to help kids find a fun way to connect with democracy and understand issues that are happening around them—and make them issues they want to contribute to solving."

3.

New Bonds in Georgia

(THE STORY OF MACON MONEY)

One of the earliest and most innovative examples of games used to inspire real-world change was the Knight Foundation's community-building social game Macon Money. The game was more of an experiment than a fully fledged undertaking, and as a result, perhaps had less impact than projects like PeaceMaker and iCivics. However, it was no less ambitious. The game was designed to revitalize downtown Macon, Georgia, in the hope of easing racial tensions and leading to a more integrated community, particularly in an area known as College Hill Corridor, Macon's main commercial strip, a boulevard connecting Mercer University to the city's civic center.

Like many cities in the country's South, Macon is largely segregated. It's not uncommon for people to live, shop, and commute exclusively alongside those of the same race, just as it's not uncommon for schools and supermarkets to be unofficially designated as black, white, or Latino. In some parts of the country, this has been traced back to decades-old housing policies that often prevented black residents from acquiring property in certain areas or neighborhoods of a town or city, a practice known as "redlining." [1]

In 2016, the Brookings Institution analyzed the Census Bureau's 2010–2014 American Community Survey[2] and found that, while black-white segregation is slowly declining in large cities, it still remains inexplicably high throughout most of the country. The 52 largest metropolitan areas—including Milwaukee, New York, Chicago, Detroit, Cleveland, and Buffalo—showed segregation levels between 50 and 70, where zero represents perfect integration and 100 represents complete segregation. "While far below the nearly apartheid racial separation that existed for much of the nation's history, these are still high measures," the report's author, William H. Frey, a senior fellow at Metropolitan Policy Program, concluded.

Things are changing—just very slowly. In 2000, the average black Chicago resident lived in a neighborhood that was 72 percent black, 17 percent white, and 8 percent Hispanic. By 2010–2014, this had shifted to 64 percent black, 19 percent white, and 12.5 percent Hispanic. In Georgia, in the Atlanta-Sandy Springs-Roswell area, the black-white segregation level decreased from 64 in 2000 to 59 in 2010–2014.

In 2008, Alberto Ibargüen, the former publisher of the *Miami Herald* and the president and CEO of the Knight Foundation, instructed a young Knight employee named Jessica Goldfin to investigate the possibility of using games to extend the reach of

Knight's community-building projects, which aim to connect residents and neighbors through the arts, media, and civics. (One of the best examples is Knight's Soul of the Community study, a three-year project, undertaken throughout 26 communities, that focused on getting residents to come together and support local businesses and initiatives.)

Goldfin began looking for examples of experimental games that had been applied in a real-world setting. "It was a medium so many people loved, and they were thinking: 'Hey, this might be a way to get young people interested in stuff,'" she told us. She came across Area/Code, a New York game studio founded by a former ad man named Kevin Slavin and the current director of the NYU Game Center, Frank Lantz. (Lantz is also a celebrated game designer. Area/Code no longer exists; it was successfully acquired by Zynga in 2011 but shut down a few years later.)

Area/Code seemed like a good place to start. The company specialized in creating games with a real-world link: an online game synchronized to a live television broadcast, for example, or a video game in which players were able to follow, in real time, the movements of six great white sharks in California via satellite tracking. One of the company's early projects involved a team-based, citywide treasure hunt designed for high school students, who were tasked with finding and photographing different items with mobile phone cameras. An online site showed each player's location as the game progressed, encouraging those who couldn't play in real life to tune in. The winning team received a $5,000 scholarship for their school.

Ibargüen hired Area/Code to design a series of games about civic engagement, which Knight could implement in its existing programs serving underdeveloped communities. The studio decided to first identify five cities in which a game like this could work and would have the most impact. The studio's executive producer, Kati London, put together a small team of researchers, game designers, and an ethnographer and began conversations with Knight program managers on the ground in different communities.

The problem was that a lot of the issues identified by the program managers didn't seem to have an obvious link to games—homelessness, for example. London decided to find a narrower focus. She took her team to visit five cities—Biloxi, Mississippi; Macon, Georgia; Lexington, Kentucky; Detroit, Michigan; and Charlotte, North Carolina. In each place she talked to the mayor, local residents, business owners, and anyone else she came across who could help her identify a local issue that might be addressed with the help of a game.

At the time, Knight's program manager for Macon was a woman named Beverly Blake, a soft-spoken 62-year-old with expressive eyes and a faint Southern accent. Blake had spent most of her life in Atlanta, where she worked in the private sector, before moving to Macon and taking a job with the Knight Foundation in 2004. She was the first person to volunteer when she found out Knight was investigating games as a way to engage Knight communities. "I saw it as an opportunity to break down barriers in the community and bring people from different neighborhoods, ages, and races together," she told us.

Blake put together a list of people in Macon who might be able to give London and her team an idea of what it's like to live in the town: high school students, Mercer University staff and professors, ministers, College Hill Corridor business owners, and so on. When London and her team arrived in Macon, Blake introduced them to everyone, from the mayor to the guy who ran the town garbage dump. "My first night there, we went to drag queen bingo downtown," London said. She spoke to students, homeowners, artists, business owners, and restaurateurs. "We needed to get the perspectives of those who weren't in power."

After weeks of canvassing, one issue kept reemerging: the problem of a brain drain. Mercer University students were moving away from the town right after graduating. No one was staying in Macon, finding a job, and settling down—probably because there were no jobs to be found. On top of that, students had no connections outside the college; there was no hanging out downtown and chatting with the locals. There seemed to be nothing in Macon that persuaded them they could have a future there. "So we thought, how could we create something that is accessible enough to give people an excuse to say hello to each other?"

London presented her findings in a report to Knight, outlining the opportunities a social game might bring to each of the five cities. People at Knight were excited. The foundation funded two pilot projects: one in Macon and another in Biloxi. (The Biloxi project ended up being a game promoting hurricane preparedness through youth-focused activities.) In Macon, Knight wanted to focus on the three zip codes tied to College Hill Corridor, the town's main commercial strip. The foundation was already in the middle of efforts to revitalize the area, and they hoped a social game could help connect Mercer students to downtown business owners and Macon residents in neighboring areas.

London now had to design a social game that could do all that.

It was agreed that the central "mechanic" of the game—now known as Macon Money—would be a Match 3 concept. Knight would print and distribute bonds, each imprinted with three different symbols, all related to Macon's history. The symbols included a peach, a kazoo, a musical note, a cherry blossom, and more. Once a player was in possession of a bond, his or her task would be to find a match: another player whose bond had the same exact three symbols. Once a match was made, players could exchange their bonds for Macon Money, an alternative currency that could be spent in participating shops and businesses downtown. These would be the equivalent of $10 or $20, sometimes $50, and occasionally $100. The businesses involved could then cash in all of their Macon Money to the Knight Foundation, which would reimburse them in full.

The Macon Money bills themselves were designed to reflect Macon's history. London's team decided they wanted the face of the great American soul singer Otis Redding on the bills. It was felt that a likeness of Redding, a Maconite respected and loved by the community, would capture the spirit of connection and friendship. (Redding's wife gave permission for the image of his face to be used. Some people who played the game, it was later discovered, loved the bills so much that they framed them instead of cashing them in.)

Knight's decision to fund a nondigital project—a physical game that would require residents of Macon to interact with each other in the real world, not just online—was a bold move. There was little data to prove that this kind of thing had worked before. Other communities had employed alternative, real-world currencies with the same purpose, but no one had used a game before.

(The BerkShares currency for the Berkshire region of Massachusetts is still used: the currency was introduced in 2006 to encourage capital to remain within the region and to build better relationships between local business owners and the community. Ithaca, New York, also continues to utilize what's known as "Ithaca Hours," the oldest local currency still operating in the US. One bill is generally equivalent to $10 and can be used to pay someone for one hour's work.)

Macon Money took nine months to build. Game designers were hired; London kept in regular touch with Blake and Macon community representatives to run ideas by them. "We'd come back with the research, summarize it, and see what there is to go after," London said. "We'd think about different game mechanics, who we were trying to reach, and how to do that in the easiest way."

The "who" was easy: college students and residents aged 18–50 in a three-zip-code area in Macon; some were permanent residents, some were downtown residents, some were business owners, and some were students. Were they already connecting with each other? Yes, through church groups and Knight-funded public concerts and social events. What were their media habits like? Most had access to Facebook and other social media, and almost everyone was reachable by mail. "For the foundation, we didn't just want to do a game for the game's sake," Goldfin said. "Social impact is hard, and takes a lot of time. If it's not owned and driven by the community, it's just not going to work."

At the same time, Knight had realistic expectations. "We didn't think this game was going to fully solve any real problems," continued Goldfin, who was eventually promoted to chief of staff of the project and worked closely with London and her team. "I think that's a problem with social-impact games—people expect them to do that, but that's not feasible. But using a game as a tactic to reinforce other activities, in a way that invites new audiences, is interesting."

The first challenge was getting around the legal definition of "game" in the state of Georgia. Was Macon Money a game of skill or a game of chance? Turns out it had to be the former, because the latter was illegal. (The foundation spent $10,000 in legal fees clearing up that little snafu.) The next thing on the list was convincing local businesses to get involved, which, at the end of the day, meant telling business owners to give up their revenue for six months and trust that Knight would reimburse them in full. At first, businesses owners were concerned that they'd have to put some of their own money into the game; then, they expressed doubt about the Knight Foundation's promise to come through with reimbursement. London: "When you're asking business owners in an impoverished city to believe that you're going to reimburse them, and you're a New York City game studio . . ."

This part was relatively easy to figure out: every month, businesses would report the amount of Macon Money they took in, and Knight would reimburse them dollar for dollar. (The Macon Money bills had serial numbers and security redundancies to ensure that they were tracked and legitimate.)

Next, it was Maconites' turn to be skeptical. A letter in the mail saying you can win money has all the marks of a shady scheme, and indeed that's what many residents thought Macon Money was at first. In order to soothe residents' worries, Knight looked for someone who could take over the day-to-day operations and who already had ties with the local community. In other words, someone people felt they could trust.

In August 2010, a local resident named Mechel McKinley was hired to coordinate all aspects of Macon Money on the ground: bond distribution, redemption, event management, public relations, website management, social media management, and, most importantly, the development and maintenance of relationships with residents and local business owners. "I was the only person on the ground, which was a good thing, in some ways, because the community needed me and trusted me. If that someone was in New York, it would have been done for."

Young, chatty, with long blonde curls, McKinley had moved to Macon four and a half years earlier with her now ex-husband, a professor at Mercer. After they divorced, he left town, but she decided to stay on. "There's a great energy there," she said. "I was part of the wave of young professionals who moved to the area. So there was a sense of 'We're going to turn this town around.'" Prior to accepting the Knight job, McKinley had worked for a local advertising agency, and she was already involved in several different community boards in town, chairing the local branch of the Komen Race for the Cure, a fund-raising fun run in support of breast cancer research, for example. "The groups of people in my circle were committed to making Macon a better place, and turning it around."

After signing on with Knight, her first move was to hire volunteers to set up Macon Money HQ in the heart of downtown—a bland-looking office with cream-colored walls and blonde wood desks. She, too, was skeptical. She didn't think anyone was going to believe her when she said she'd be giving people free money. Another issue was the contract: because money had to change hands, Knight and Area/Code required all business owners who wanted to participate in Macon Money to sign an eight-page contract, which basically said that, yes, the owners would be re-paid in full if they chose to participate in the six-month social-game experiment known as Macon Money. McKinley talked to local business owners to persuade them to sign. "They had to trust me that I wasn't going to screw them over," McKinley said.

The problem was that the contract "was eight pages long and in 10-point type and [had] lots and lots of legalese," McKinley recalled. "And for the most part, we were dealing with small busi-ness owners, some on their own, some with just two or three employees, who just didn't have time to read this. They can like me all they want to, but when it came to this, they were like, 'Whatever, Mechel.'" McKinley kept asking London to cut down on the contract, but that never happened, she said. So she intensified her campaign, visiting businesses daily, arranging fol-low-up phone calls, even organizing small events once Macon Money officially kicked off, in October 2010, so people could see the game in action.

The first people to sign up for Macon Money were McKin-ley's friends and colleagues. McKinley took to setting up a stall on street corners to try to get people involved. "I had a folding table, a crate, and a laptop bag." She said there was a slight dis-connect between her operations on the ground and those at Knight and Area/Code. "There were ideas, but the logistics often didn't work out. At one point, there was going to be a giant acrylic box that I was supposed to carry from event to event so people could see the bonds. How am I, a human being with no staff, and a newborn, supposed to move this giant thing around town?"

Slowly, more people began signing up. Macon Money HQ was now getting daily visitors who asked for bonds. Once the game began, the bonds were distributed among the residents and business owners around College Hill Corridor, either through direct mail or at community events organized by Knight. It was McKinley who suggested that Knight didn't need to create any extra events for Macon Money—that using the existing community events, such as Second Sunday, a free music concert series held in Washington Park, would be the best way to engage residents who already knew about Macon Money and felt comfortable participating. "I'd take the game out to events, to different restaurants, community events, the Mercer cafeteria, churches . . . everywhere." (It was later revealed the highest numbers of matches were made at Second Sunday and a Knight-organized event called Third Thursday, in Mercer Village, which proved a hit with the college kids.)

Macon Money officially ended in April 2011. Overall, 48 different local businesses participated. (The initial goal was around 20.) Some businesses actually used Macon Money to launch—London remembers a chicken wings restaurant, a new bar, and a hair salon opening during the game. Local radio DJs organized flash mobs and encouraged residents to turn up and make their bond matches.

For McKinley, the best part was hearing players' stories of how they went about finding their matches. The game encouraged people to use social media like Facebook and Twitter as well as the Macon Money website forums. But some took more creative approaches, like putting their bonds in the windows of their cars and driving around town. Others advertised on community bulletin boards. Since the aim of the game was to get people to meet and talk to each other and get to know the local businesses around College Hill Corridor, Knight encouraged players to spend their Macon Money alongside their matches, which McKinley said happened often: people would come into Macon Money HQ with the people who held their matches, exchange their bonds for Macon Money, and then have coffee or lunch downtown with their match partners. Others saved their Macon Money and spent it on dinner or a special night out with their partners or families. The college kids spent Macon Money on pizza. "I remember one lady who used her Macon money on a layaway plan for a bike for her son for Christmas," McKinley said. "She was a single mom at the time, and her son was in elementary school." London: "We were trying to create as little social friction as possible—to make that effort and give people the opportunity to still say hi to each other, regardless of whether they had a match or not, without any awkwardness."

The end goal, aside from creating ties within the Macon community and easing racial tensions in town, was to quantify the impact that a social game like Macon Money could have. Knight meticulously collected data throughout the entire six months, tracking bonds and bills with serial numbers as well as traffic numbers on the Macon Money website, keeping track of foot traffic at Macon Money HQ, and seeing who was redeeming what, and how often. There were pictures of every match that was made.

An advisory board was put together to help with the evaluation of the game. Benjamin Stokes, one of the co-founders of Games for Change, was the first to join. "The conclusion was that there was no standard evaluation firm who could take this on," he said recently. "The firms that were good at community impact evaluation didn't have games expertise." Knight eventually hired Network Impact, an evaluation firm with experience in supporting nonprofits on policies surrounding immigrant integration, homelessness, and place-based civic engagement.

Madeleine Taylor, Network's founder and CEO, and her senior consultant, Anne Whatley, distributed surveys, organized individual and focus group interviews in Macon with residents and business owners who had participated in the game, and tracked down matches to see if the two individuals had stayed in touch after redeeming their bonds. "We had no idea what we'd find," Taylor said. "This had never really been tried before."

The evaluation consisted of a pregame survey sent to players after they had agreed to participate and a follow-up survey sent two months after the game ended. Taylor's favorite question in the survey was, "Would you say 'hi' if you saw your match in the street or in the supermarket?" A large proportion of players answered yes. "It's interesting because knowing a neighbor by sight correlates with social trust."

The evaluation revealed that more than 3,500 residents of Macon played Macon Money and more than 1,200 players made at least one match.[3] (Macon's total population in 2011 was just over 91,500.) Some residents played multiple times, making as many as seven matches. Network Impact concluded that the game had been a success. Overall, people's motivations for playing the game seemed to have changed over time. At first, people participated primarily because the game involved free money. From there, motivations evolved according to the individual. For one young mother who didn't get out of the house much, Macon Money was an opportunity to socialize and meet other young mothers in the community. Some of the students who played just wanted to get in the spirit of the game and make as many matches as they could, riding their bikes and skateboards down College Hill Corridor while waving their bonds above their heads. Others liked the game simply because it made them appreciate Macon more. Macon Money brought foot traffic to an otherwise bland part of town. One restaurant owner watched as Macon Money players came into his eatery and used the currency to buy meals for each other. Students would sometimes run into the restaurant with their arms draped over each other, shouting, "I got my match and I got my money and I'm paying for the whole table."

The evaluation report also included some surprising findings. Most players surveyed—nearly 80 percent—were 40 years old or younger and employed full-time, with yearly incomes of $60,000 and above. The majority were women—some 70 percent. The participants played mostly with friends, colleagues, and members of community groups, such as church groups. The game created new connections among Macon residents: 66 percent of matches were residents who did not know each other before the game began. Many players said they recognized their matches on the street later on and said hello, even though the official finding was that only one in five matches led to further personal contact, and only 15 percent of those actually friended one another on Facebook. Still, Taylor sees this as a success, since the point of the game was to get people to meet each other, not to create long-lasting relationships among residents. (As nice as that might have been.) "The proportions are small, but the pattern is significant," Network's report read. "From this we must assume that the game gave rise to what some social network analysts call 'weak ties,' and that some of these were between people of different backgrounds. Social network research shows that weak ties often provide access to new ideas, information and connections."

"[My match] actually rode down on a bicycle," one Maconite said. "I'm like, it's going to be someone that is completely out of this world! And sure enough, she wasn't American—she's Indian. Then [I find out that] we are both taking some law classes. And we were both struggling and struggling. And I said, 'You know what? Let's get this group together and let's form a study group.' And that's how it went really. My wife and I, we all had dinner and stuff like that. It was a good time." Another player described how she had befriended an African-American woman from the opposite side of town. The two are Facebook friends now. "Never in a million years would we have met. [It turned out] she went to my rival high school. So we laughed and talked about how it was when we were in high school . . . and how times have changed."

Some 92 percent of players surveyed said they had returned to new businesses they had not visited prior to the game (thus fulfilling Macon Money's aim to create more businesses in the College Hill Corridor), while 85 percent of players said that their perceptions of shops, parks, and other amenities in the downtown area had improved significantly since they started playing the game. One resident put it this way: "I mean you have the North Macon group, you have the South Macon group and you have the downtown Macon group. And usually they don't mix. . . . One of the things that Macon Money did was it encouraged them to come down and at least *see* Mercer Village. And once they came down, I think most of them were happy. . . . It gave people a reason to come back."

The key lesson of Macon Money, Network told Knight, was that a social game of its scale is best suited to a small city or neighborhood with a strong, established community, and that the game should be played intermittently, not continuously, so people don't get bored. And, perhaps most importantly, games like Macon Money cannot function on their own—they need to be part of bigger efforts to improve life for residents in the target community. (Knight was already doing this, of course. Macon was already part of the foundation's Soul of the Community project, mentioned at the start of the chapter.)

Stokes, who is now an assistant professor at American University focusing on civic media and game design, said that the evaluation could have gone further. For example, after the game concluded, Knight didn't email any of the players to share the results of the evaluation. "I would argue that people played the game as much to improve their community as for personal gain. So there really should have been feedback."

The other flaw, according to Stokes, was that while Macon Money was intended as a marketing and cultural intervention, to connect people in Macon, one of the things the game did successfully was to inject a giant sum of cash into the Macon economy, directly targeting a small area within College Hill Corridor—a rare achievement from an economic standpoint and one that Knight should have pursued further. "As a country, we are eager to find solutions for things like gentrification and homelessness,

but we don't have a lot of economic tools to fight that stuff. Macon Money had the potential to be one such tool. It was interesting as an innovation in economic development."

The game also did little to impact Macon's segregation. At the
time that Macon Money was introduced, black residents comprised 66 percent of Macon's population, and white residents
30 percent; of those who played Macon Money, only 16 percent
were black. Considering that one of the aims of the game was to
show residents from lower socioeconomic areas that downtown
wasn't just for rich white people, this is a concern.

McKinley knew that the three zip codes designated for Macon Money were not necessarily the most diverse in town. She
also knew that, as a white woman, she'd have little luck gaining
the trust of black residents and business owners. "I think if I'd
been able to go to an event at every single recreation center, or to
the more socioeconomically depressed areas of town . . . or even
if I could have hired someone with existing ties to the black
community—that would have helped immensely." It wasn't as if
people from outside the three zip codes didn't want to participate;
McKinley got regular phone calls and emails from residents asking why they hadn't been included.

Stokes said that Knight picked up, early in the game, on the
fact that the black community was underrepresented; the foundation then renewed its efforts at direct mailing of bonds to addresses
in predominantly black parts of the neighborhoods. Had they not
done this, the number of black players would have been even
lower. Had McKinley and her volunteers been able to distribute
bonds only physically, at events like Second Sunday, for example,

it's likely that 100 percent of Macon Money players would have been white.

While the evaluation report and the entire Macon Money structure is available online for anyone to download, the idea that a social game of this size, and with such lofty impact goals, could work anywhere with minimal effort seems naïve. One of the first cities to approach Knight with the idea of replicating Macon Money was Boston. There was a lot of enthusiasm on both sides, but things quickly fell apart when it became clear that no one in the Boston mayor's office was willing to dedicate the time and resources to a project of this size. "It's not just a board game where you can take it out, read the instructions, and go," Goldfin said. "It's more of a heavy lift." Even if everything is well documented, the game requires someone to push it along, sustain it, and work out how exactly it fits into the local community. Goldfin continued: "It's a lot of talking to people, keeping the buzz and momentum up. Even [Boston], who were savvier, and using more innovative tools [than we did in Macon], realized it was going to be a lot of work."

Money is another potential issue. Macon Money was successful because the Knight Foundation pumped a significant amount of money into the project, something that not every community will be able to do. According to Stokes, Knight was wrong to conceive Macon Money's legacy as a DIY toolkit. "It's like saying, I want cities all around the country to have more parks, so I'll make a toolkit that shows cities how to build parks. And then asking, 'Why are all these poor communities not making parks? I showed them how to do it!'" Macon Money is a social intervention aimed at achieving a major outcome; still, it works only if there is a base level of investment. Stokes said that Knight could have been clearer on what kind of communities could benefit from games like this: those, say, with an existing business corridor and a close-knit community. "We're at a cultural moment where we're just considering games this way. And only just getting to a moment where this is becoming a possibility."

Sarah Gerwig-Moore, co-chair of the College Hill Corridor Commission during Macon Money, helped advise London and her team on the best approach to the game. A lawyer, she grew up in Macon, attended Mercer, then moved away to live in London and San Francisco before returning to Macon to teach law at Mercer. She said that while some of the businesses that participated in Macon Money have since closed, the effects of the game on the community have been huge. "Sure, it didn't solve our race problem, but the momentum it brought with it was significant to the area changing," she said, speaking on the phone from a coffee shop in downtown Macon.

"I'm sitting outside a coffee shop within two blocks of my house. When I moved here eight years ago, this was an abandoned strip of land. It was a target for crime; there were no streetlights, no trees. Now, sitting here, I can see a pizza place, an organic sandwich shop, and a bookstore, all within walking distance. The park I can see from where I'm sitting has attracted hundreds of thousands of dollars of redevelopment money—there are new tennis courts, new fountains, and new pathways. The optimism Macon Money brought to the community is responsible for a lot."

PART II

FROM JEDDAH TO NAIROBI

Games that Explore Pressing Social Issues from Around the World.

4.

A Prince's Tale

(THE STORY OF NEW ARAB MEDIA)

I f you believe what you read, Saudi Arabia's Prince Fahad bin Faisal Al Saud has been a busy royal. The 32-year-old grandson of King Salman's older brother, the late Crown Prince Sultan bin Abdulaziz Al Saud, was allegedly spotted celebrating his graduation in May 2013 at Disneyland Paris, where Agence France-Press reported that he reserved entire areas of the park for three straight days, during which he and 60 guests managed to blow 15 million euros on lavish, tailor-made events.[1] In 2014, Prince Fahad also reportedly traveled to Pakistan for a three-week safari to hunt the endangered Houbara bustard bird.[2]

Except that Prince Fahad wasn't in Disneyland, or in Pakistan. Several European news sites mistakenly published photos of Prince Fahad when reporting on the Disneyland debacle, which was, allegedly, the debacle of a different prince, Prince Fahd Al-Saud. In

the case of the Houbara bird, the prince responsible was reportedly Prince Fahd bin Abdul Sultan bin Abdul Aziz Al Saud.[3] "I
was in Jordan, and a random girl came up to me in a bar and asked,
'Aren't you the guy who spent $20 million in Disneyland?'" Fa-
had told us recently. "I was like, 'Girl, if I had $20 million do you
really think I'd be standing here talking to you?'"

We were at a tea parlor in east London, part of Shoreditch
House, the city's members-only hangout for celebrities, socialites
and princes alike. Fahad was in town to shoot a video promo for
his start-up, New Arab Media (NA3M), a digital media company
focused on using pop culture—specifically, comic books, films,
and video games—to shift long-standing Western perceptions of
the Arab world. (In Arabic, "NA3M" translates to a positive af-
firmation, like "yes!")

The company has already made and released a number of successful mobile games for the Arab-speaking market. But it's an
ambitious, yet-to-be-released video game, comic-book series,
and accompanying universe called Saudi Girls Revolution (SGR)
that Fahad believes will turn NA3M into a household name.
SGR is about a group of renegade Saudi Arabian women who
ride motorcycles and dispatch their adversaries in style.

Fahad hopes the game and accompanying comic book will
give Arabic-speaking youth worldwide a group of superheroes
with whom they identify: figures rooted in Arab culture and my-
thology, rather than appropriated from Western pop culture. If
Arab kids grow up seeing themselves represented in popular culture, for example—not as stereotypes but as richly drawn
characters—then perhaps they'll grow up envisioning a world full
of possibilities.

By the same token, if American kids grow up playing games like SGR, where Arab culture is celebrated rather than stereotyped, then perhaps they will grow up to be more understanding of the world, and more tolerant.

"I want young Arabs to play SGR and think, 'Yeah! Look at us!'" Fahad said, pumping the air. "But I also want young Westerners to play it and think, 'This is unlike anything I've ever seen before.'"

FAHAD IS TALL, BEARDED, and well-mannered. To say he's an eccentric dresser is an understatement: on the day of our meeting, he was sporting an oversized black T-shirt made out of wetsuit material, and silky black shorts that wouldn't have looked out of place in a Rick Owens ready-to-wear collection. He grew up in Jeddah, a port city on the Red Sea, 900 kilometers southwest of Riyadh, Saudi's capital. He says that most people imagine his childhood was like something in the Eddie Murphy film *Coming to America*, when in reality it had more in common with *Family Ties*.

When Fahad's father was young, he chose to forgo his inheritance in favor of starting his own business. He began with real estate and eventually moved into fiber optics. After he married Fahad's mother, the couple lived in a small apartment above the company office. "Every month, my mother would sell part of her jewelry to support him," Fahad said. She, too, was against the idea of inheriting rather than earning. Part of the first generation of Saudi women allowed to attend school, she studied anthropology and business at university before starting her own business.

When Fahad was young, the family moved away from the

capital. Fahad's mother wanted her children to grow up away from any associations with extravagance. The family lived in a modest house—technically called a "palace," but far from most people's idea of one. (Fahad concedes that there was a nice pool, however.)

Fahad began working at his mother's company at 14, getting coffee and running minor errands. He also washed cars, picked up groceries, and did the washing up at home. At 17, he announced that he wanted to move to the United States. "While my parents were investing in physical infrastructure, I was living in the digital world. I wanted to study at Stanford and get involved in the tech world."

Fahad wanted to study electrical engineering at Stanford, but he figured he'd work his way up to that goal. He applied to UCLA and was accepted. He packed his bags and arrived in the US on September 10, 2001. The next morning, he woke up to a frantic phone call from his sister. "Are you seeing this?" she cried. He turned on the television and watched as the second plane hit the World Trade Center.

Over the next few days, he watched as news reports detailed a mounting wave of hate crimes against Muslims throughout the country. On September 13, Fahad said he received an email from UCLA. "They said they couldn't ensure my safety and that I would be a liability," he said. "They didn't exactly tell me to leave, but the meaning was clear."

On September 15, 2001, Fahad returned to Saudi Arabia. His parents were relieved, but he was restless. "I took 9/11 as a personal attack on my future and my education." The following year, he sent his application to Stanford and was accepted. He flew back to the United States, telling his parents that he was going only for an interview and that he'd be back soon. They didn't learn the truth until some months later. Angry, they deployed his uncle to California to bring Fahad back. Instead, the uncle was impressed. Fahad had acclimatized to life at Stanford. He'd switched from electrical engineering to mechanical engineering. He'd been invited to join a fraternity. "Some kids rebel by getting a tattoo. I rebelled by getting into Stanford," Fahad joked.

There weren't many other Arab undergrads at Stanford at the time. Fahad would occasionally hear of Arab students being plucked out and having their visas revoked. So he kept a low profile. He didn't drink. He didn't party. He didn't go on spring break. Instead, he joined an a cappella group. Other students thought he was African, and he didn't correct them. He was invited to join Sigma Nu, a progressive fraternity that was once banned in 1963 for defying official fraternity bylaws and accepting an African-American student.[4]

While Fahad was at Stanford, some of his friends graduated and moved on to work at Facebook. As the social network's reach grew, the company began getting requests from business owners in Saudi Arabia and Egypt who wanted to build profiles on Facebook but needed a translation service. One of Fahad's friends who worked at the company asked if Fahad would be interested in contributing to that service. He helped out once or twice, but then joked that if he was going to keep doing it, he might as well be getting paid for it. His friend organized an interview, and after graduating, Fahad began working in Facebook's customer service department for $21/hour, resetting passwords for Arabic customers. "I remember asking in my interview if I had to cut my hair. I said if I had to, I didn't think I could work there. And the dude started laughing and said, 'Well, your manager has pink hair, so I think you'll be fine.'"

Two weeks into the job, he found himself at a company meeting with Mark Zuckerberg. He'd never seen the Facebook CEO before and was taken aback. "I saw this young kid with red hair, and I'm like, 'Who is this guy?'" Zuckerberg talked about Facebook's growth around the world. But there was no mention of the Middle East. Fahad knew the social network was already popular in Arab countries—he had the stats to prove it. So he stood up and asked Zuckerberg, "Why not the Middle East?" According to Fahad, Zuckerberg's response was something like, "Because it's too risky and they have bad internet service."

Zuckerberg moved on, but Fahad cut him off. "I said, 'Hold on, I'm not done yet. I'm from the [Middle East], and that was an ignorant, typically American thing to say.'" Fahad then pointed to his data suggesting the increasing adoption of Facebook in the Middle East. He also pointed to the fact that young people were rapidly becoming the dominant demographic in Saudi Arabia.[5] "I got a standing ovation," he said. After that, he was made head of the User Operations Arabic department—a one-man operation tasked with coordinating the growth of Facebook in the Middle East. After the launch of Facebook Arabic, user numbers rose across 23 Arabic-speaking countries. By 2009, Facebook had 900,000 users in Egypt, 250,000 users in Saudi Arabia, and 300,000 users in Lebanon.[6]

A year later, the Arab Spring began.

FAHAD OFTEN FLIES BACK to Saudi Arabia to perform various royal duties: usually attending state celebrations or funerals. He's been settling tribal wars and holding religious symposiums since he was 15—the threshold of adulthood for young Saudi men. "It was a little weird, sure, to be so young and yet responsible for so much," he says. "All I wanted to do was go back into my room and play video games." Fahad's mother once told him to think of his title as a job he was born with. When the new Saudi king assumed power, in 2015, Fahad attended the ceremony, to pledge allegiance on his family's behalf.

In 2011, Fahad left Facebook to join the Saudi Arabian Foreign Ministry as the head of student affairs at the Saudi embassy in Los Angeles. By then, he had already been married and divorced. He met his wife, also a Saudi student, while at Stanford. "We were young—too young. We were learning about each other as we were living with each other. There was no dating period. It was straight into life, stress, jobs, and bills."

A lot of this had to do with cultural pressure. In Saudi Arabia, married men and women command much more respect than their unmarried siblings or cousins. Both Fahad and his wife understood this, but living in the United States had changed their perspective somewhat. They decided to split amicably and filed for divorce. Fahad's parents were despondent. "They saw it as a failure," he said. He viewed it as a lesson.

At the Saudi embassy, Fahad consulted with universities in both Saudi Arabia and the United States to develop a support network of banks and lawyers for the growing number of Saudi students coming to the US to study. A recent expansion of Saudi Arabia's scholarship program meant that by 2011, there were around 150,000 Saudis studying around the world; about a third of those were in the United States.[7] "These kids were being plucked out of villages in Saudi Arabia and thrown into schools in New York and San Francisco," Fahad says. "They had no idea what to expect."

Ten years after 9/11, incidents of Islamophobia continued unabated across the United States. After hate crimes against people of Middle Eastern descent increased from 354 attacks in 2000 to 1,501 attacks in 2001,[8] new reports surfaced detailing accounts of thousands of Muslim, South Asian, and Middle Eastern men detained by the FBI, police, and immigration officers.

"The neighborhoods were in a state of virtual lockdown, with women afraid to venture out to the grocery store or to send their children to school," as one report from 2006 described the situation.[9] "The FBI began randomly interviewing thousands of men with Muslim names, creating further panic. Arrests were made on the basis of tips and reports of 'suspicious activity.' Most of the arrests took place between 2am and 6am and the 'midnight knock' came to be dreaded."

In 2013, a Saudi student from Michigan made headlines after an innocent stroll across his university campus with a rice cooker led someone to call the police.[10] "That should give you an idea of the kind of climate we were dealing with," Fahad says.

Fahad says that one morning during his junior year at Stanford, the FBI showed up at his brother's house in the Los Altos hills with eight cars. "I used to stay there sometimes on weekends, and they came searching for someone who used to work with me and my brother—a former assistant. He was let go and reentered the US on his previous visa, and his last known address was this house." Fahad says he told the FBI to get a warrant and informed the Saudi embassy of what had happened. A few years later, while he was married and living in Los Angeles, Fahad says representatives of the US Department of Homeland Security showed up at his house looking for his brother-in-law, who had passed away from a heart attack a few months previously. "They came to our apartment and started harassing us," he says. "So I set up a meeting with my lawyers and asked them what they wanted. They confessed they were looking for a person of interest—my brother-in-law. I told them he was six feet under. His death certificate was public record." (Neither the FBI nor the Department of Homeland Security responded to a request for comment.)

Fahad stopped visiting his parents in Saudi Arabia. He spoke with an American accent when he went through immigration at US airports. He even dyed his hair lighter. "As an Arab in a post 9/11 world, I needed to at least pass for Mexican," he jokes.

Eventually, he decided to do something about it.

WHILE THE MIDDLE EAST still has a relatively low internet adoption rate—53 percent compared with the US at 88 percent, Western Europe at 83 percent, South America at 60 percent, and East Asia at 54 percent—the region is quickly catching up.[11] In 2014, internet adoption was highest in Qatar, Bahrain, and the United Arab Emirates (UAE), all around 90 percent. Saudi Arabia ranked somewhere in the middle, with around 64 percent.

Internet-enabled phones are helping: according to one report, the number of mobile phone subscriptions in the Middle East increased from 20 million to 54 million between 2006 and 2011.[12] In 2013, a research firm conducted a study in six countries—Saudi Arabia, Egypt, Jordan, the UAE, Lebanon, and Kuwait—with more than 22,000 participants answering questions about their daily internet and mobile phone habits. The study found that Saudi Arabia and the UAE have the highest rates of smartphone penetration, at 63 percent and 61 percent, respectively.[13] "Pretty much every Saudi has at least two smartphones: one iOS, and one Android," Fahad says.

Music, games, and video are the three most downloaded types of online content in the region. Saudi Arabia has highest rate of online television watching across internet users, at 25 percent. Jordan has the highest rate of electronic game use across the Middle Eastern entire population, at 40 percent. The region's tech-adoption rate also extends to social media—Saudi is frequently cited as one of the largest adopters of Twitter in the Arab world, accounting for around 40 percent of all active Twitter users in the region. (That's 2.4 million active users in Saudi Arabia alone.)[14]

One likely reason for Saudi Arabia's accelerated online growth is the country's predominantly young demographic; according to recent reports,[15] some 70 percent of the country's population is under the age of 30. "Clearly, the Arab awakening is shifting the region's political center of gravity from an older to a younger generation," wrote Pulitzer Prize–winning journalist Carlyle Murphy, who spent three years living and working in Saudi Arabia. "All of a sudden, the youth of the Arab world are front and center in everyone's consciousness."

The downside is that a lot of young Saudis get bored easily. There are no cinemas in Saudi Arabia, and minimal outdoor activities or social clubs; youth are generally expected to spend most of their time at home, with their families.

It's not hard to see why social media and smartphones are

now the primary tools for both communication and distraction for many young Saudis. "People went from no infrastructure to flat screens," Fahad says.

In 2012, Fahad went back home, with the intention of founding a tech start-up that would provide jobs for young people in the Middle East while incubating, producing, and distributing art, comic books, and video games to challenge Western stereotypes of the region. He knew the market well: he'd grown up on games like Street Fighter, Fatal Fury, Samurai Showdown, Super Mario Bros, Sonic, and Kirby. He figured that since everyone in the region had a smartphone, and people's attention spans would likely keep getting shorter, mobile gaming was a good starting point.

But first, he needed to learn on the job. He invested in a company called Popover Games, which was trying to create digital versions of old Arabic card games that didn't exist on Facebook. He eventually took over as co-founder, but the company failed to take off and was later sold. He then partnered with two friends to start a mobile app development company called Appiphany, which created apps like InstaFeed, an app that lets Instagram users divide followers into different categories and channels. That eventually folded too—mostly due to changing visions. "It happens, one friend decided he wanted to open a Crossfit gym, the other wanted to get married. I had a plan of wanting to change perceptions of the Arab world. So, you know, we just ended up having different goals."

In 2013, Fahad founded New Arab Media (NA3M). He invested his own money in the venture—mostly because he didn't want to answer to anyone else, but also because Saudi investors tend to be a notoriously cautious bunch who expect Wall Street–sized returns on every investment. An entertainment media company run by a Saudi royal would raise some eyebrows. It didn't help that failure is not an acceptable outcome in Saudi culture; that applies to everything from personal matters to business.

It took a year for Fahad to put together an initial team. NA3M's first game, an Arabic educational language game for mobiles and tablets called Let's Go Alphabet, was a hit. The game went to number one among app stores in Egypt, Saudi Arabia, Jordan, the UAE, Morocco, and Kuwait. (The game is animal-themed. Every time young players draw a letter successfully, they unlock a new animal to play with and advance to the next stage.)

Although the game did well, Fahad says he encountered a lot of skepticism. While young people in the Middle East have grown up with video games and comics, they have always been American video games and comics. "We didn't get stuff in categories— it was just 'American stuff,'" Fahad says. "Picture a bunch of macho Saudi guys dancing to the Spice Girls, and you get the idea."

Fahad says the merits of a particular game or song or film are not really discussed. It's either American or it isn't. A mobile phone game made in the Middle East, with Middle Eastern themes, still feels strange. "There isn't a lot of good, high-quality Arabic content, so we immediately had to match the American quality and compete with the entire global mobile phone game market. We were making our first mobile game, and we had to make it good enough that it could compete with the likes of Disney."

NA3M's second mobile game, Run Camel Run, was also successful, making it into the top five on the Saudi app store, next to the sleeper hit Flappy Bird. This time, the game was aimed at adult players. It's a retro-inspired free runner/platforming game about a camel named Faisal who must run across the rooftops of cities like Riyadh and Paris collecting coins and avoiding enemies.

In 2013, NA3M opened its first office in Jordan, and a year later, an office in Copenhagen. Jordan was the obvious choice for a home base in the Middle East: tech is one of Jordan's fastest-growing industries, led, in large part, by King Abdullah II of Jordan, who has encouraged outside investment in the sector and supported programs and partnerships that propel tech development in the region. During 2011 and 2012, Jordan was one of the leading Middle Eastern countries for tech deals funded.[16] By 2013, more than 600 tech companies had been formed in the country, leading to the creation of some 84,000 jobs and making up 12 percent of the country's gross domestic product. Jordan's capital, Amman, is now considered among the top ten cities in the world to start a tech company.

"I can't tell you what Syria will look like politically in a year, or Saudi and Iran in three, but I can tell you with 100 percent certainty that two-thirds of humanity will have a smart device by the end of this decade," said Christopher Schroeder, author of *Startup Rising—The Entrepreneurial Revolution Remaking the Middle East.*

Perhaps the best example is the Arab internet services company Maktoob, founded in Jordan, which sold to Yahoo! for $164 million in 2009. A former auction site linked to Maktoob, Souq .com, is now the largest e-commerce site in the Arab world and is often referred to as the Amazon of the Middle East. "I may start calling it the Maktoob effect now," Schroeder joked.

"[Our people] are young, aspiring, and globally aware," Jordan's monarch told the "Innovative Jordan" conference at the University of California Berkeley.[17] "They are active users of the internet, social media, and new technology. They know regional demand for content, apps, and platforms—indeed, they are helping to drive that demand."

Gaming companies are catching on. In October 2015, Alain Corre, an executive at Ubisoft, spoke about the video game publisher's decision to open studios in both Abu Dhabi and Casablanca and localize a number of Ubisoft titles for the Arabic-speaking market. "There are 420 million people in the region, making it a bigger potential market than the US and Europe," Corre told the video game website IGN. "More and more people in the region also are playing video games. One consultancy recently predicted that by 2022 the Middle East video game market would triple from what it is today to become a $4.4 billion opportunity."

NA3M now employs around 30 people across its two locations, from 16 different nationalities. On a recent Sunday afternoon, we Skyped with India Alston and Jude Soub, NA3M's marketing director and community manager, respectively. Alston met Fahad at Stanford, where she was pursuing African-American studies. The two stayed in touch, and when Alston founded a small marketing consultancy firm in Washington, DC, in 2010, Fahad called to tell her about NA3M. "I saw it as a moving train headed somewhere important," she said. "And I wanted to be there when it arrived." She relocated to Denmark and then to Amman. She helps coordinate social media, public relations, marketing, and sponsorship for the company. "We see people embracing Asian culture, African-American culture, Latino culture. But there is a great misconception about Arab culture."

Soub is Jordanian. While studying in Boston, she witnessed Western ignorance firsthand. "People would walk up to me and ask me, in all seriousness, stuff like, 'Did you live in a tent?' and 'Did you go to school on a camel?'" She says the rapid growth of the technology sector in Jordan has attracted the interest of a lot of young women who grew up on a steady diet of social media, You-Tube, and video games.

"It used to be that you had to become either a lawyer, a doctor, or an engineer," she said. "But that's changing. Women are now coming to tech and art."

A FEW DAYS AFTER our meeting at Shoreditch House, we met up with Fahad inside a large Georgian townhouse in London's swish Kensington neighborhood, where the NA3M promo was being filmed. "This is an Airbnb, by the way," Fahad said. "Just before you go thinking I own this place or something." (He had just moved to Berlin.)

Fahad revised his notes as the camera crew set up. "You know, 'Fahad' actually means 'cheetah' in Arabic," he said. One of his key advisors, Rozan Ahmed, looked up. "I think it actually means 'leopard,'" she said. Fahad nodded. "It's kind of interchangeable. But I like cheetah better. Faster, more powerful."

When the cameras rolled, Fahad talked about giving young Arabs a voice. "We have made nine games in two years. Some have hit number one. Some haven't. But they've all been about our region—our culture and our values. We're representing and presenting the Middle East in a way that's never been witnessed before."

Later, Fahad confessed that his faith in technology also comes from the fact that it transcends religious boundaries, which he says are "created by mass media to divide and confuse . . . There's no scripture in the Koran that says, 'Do not send that text message.'" He went on: "I'm a Muslim. But I'm also a human being. That means that I have a brain, and I have my own experiences. No other entity can stand between my mind and the contents of our holy scripture—or any holy scripture. I follow my faith in a way that makes sense to me at this point, rather than just blindly following the flock, or believing the misinformed agendas of a news station."

Saudi Girls Revolution was inspired by a similar realization. When Fahad returned to Saudi Arabia in 2012, he read about the growing movement among those protesting the ban on female drivers in the country. There's no official law against women driving in Saudi Arabia—the government simply refuses to issue permits to female drivers. It's more like a deeply ingrained societal norm in which, as with all aspects of Saudi life, the fear of bringing shame upon one's family overrides any liberal-minded attempts at progress. And yet, on October 26, 2013, more than 60 Saudi women drove in public to protest the ban[18]; it was, at the time, the largest public demonstration of solidarity by Saudi women.

When Western media outlets cover Saudi women's rights, the driving ban is usually the first thing mentioned (sometimes it's the only thing). But as Fahad spoke to women around him, he realized that the issue was more complicated. Yes, there were women in Saudi who wanted to drive. But it wasn't exactly at the top of their list in terms of personal freedoms. "I talked to women with PhDs, who are well educated and liberal—and a lot of them said they don't care about driving, as much as they do about education, for example," Fahad said. "Driving was not their main or absolute concern. They want legal rights. They want to travel on their own. They want to have stronger positions in business, social reform, and in politics."

Saudi Arabia practices strict gender segregation in most public places—schools, restaurants, mosques, and even inside the home. The guardianship system means women require a male guardian's consent to study, travel, or work. A Saudi woman cannot leave the house without a full-length abaya, which covers her head and body. In recent years, a growing number of women, especially younger women, have pushed aggressively for reforms. And for the most part, it's worked. In June 2011, the late King Abdullah issued a decree that effectively allowed Saudi women to join the wider workforce, stating that women had to replace all men working in lingerie shops. (At the time, almost all Saudi women in the workforce were employed in schools or hospitals, teaching and attending to female students and patients.) In 2013, supermarkets began hiring female employees for the first time.[19] That same year, the first Saudi female lawyers—four in total— were granted practicing certificates. By 2015, the number of Saudi women working had increased by 48 percent, representing about 16 percent of the total workforce.[20] By 2016, close to 70 women had been granted certificates to practice law, and over half of the country's university students were female.

In 2011, King Abdullah endorsed a female-led campaign demanding the right to vote, announcing that he would allow women to run as candidates and to vote in the 2015 elections.[21] He also appointed 30 women to the 150-member Majlis Al Shura, the kingdom's top advisory body. Since then, women have been working from the inside to change the system. Many young women now demand that their marriage contracts include clauses guaranteeing their husbands' consent for the wives' finishing their education or pursuing work. They are lobbying for tougher punishments for domestic abuse and changes to current divorce laws, which strongly favor men. (Under some interpretations of Islamic law, it is possible for a man to divorce his wife by simply saying "I divorce you" three times.[22] A woman, on the other hand, usually requires the agreement of a Muslim judge.) When the 2015 elections rolled around, 978 women registered as candidates (alongside just under 6,000 men), and 130,000 women turned out to vote.[23]

In late 2015, Saudi Arabia announced the introduction of reforms allowing divorced women and widows to manage their own family affairs without prior approval from male guardians or judges.[24] Previously, divorced women and widows would have had to ask permission from their former husbands or a court if they wished to do simple things like enroll their children in school or go to a hospital. "If you asked me which was more important, this or driving, I would tell you a hundred times this," Salwa al-Hazza, a member of the Shura council, told the *Guardian* in 2015. "It gives [a Saudi woman] the right to identify herself as head of the family, to put her children through school, get them married."

"The coming decade in Saudi Arabia will be marked by clashes of gender expectations in both society at large and in individual families, as young women demanding greater freedom and opportunities come up against still-dominant patriarchal attitudes," Murphy wrote. "It is very difficult to have a creative, dynamic, and productive economic system if half the population is segregated."

When Fahad first showed his mother and sister the concept art for SGR's universe, they advised him to be cautious. Particularly about the title—something about putting the words "Saudi," "girls," and "revolution" together might lead some more conservative minds to misconstrue Fahad's true intentions for the project. "Anything in the Middle East that goes against this falsified Western grain is seen as political," he says. "But SGR isn't a political move at all. It's a social one. It's entertainment. Our general view of women, internationally, has to change. Women are the driving force of all culture, education, and stability—my own mother and both grand-mothers proved that to me. But for the most part, women are beaten down by entertainment. Degraded and sexually ex-ploited. Why is that okay? We know art can influence society and that's what we're dedicated to. I'm not here trying to change people's views so much as simply to challenge them."

SGR will use multiple platforms to tell one story. The first "season" will be a digital comic book, released in nine issues. It will establish the story of eight Saudi women in a post-apocalyptic world struggling against a hyper-patriarchy bent on enslaving and brutalizing women. Each character represents a different Saudi de-mographic: one character is mixed-race; another is gay. One is a cyborg. (She represents women who are viewed by Saudi society as "broken"—either divorced or past the culturally accepted age for marriage.) There are two twins, as well as a priestess with fair skin and hair, who represents the privileged youth of Saudi.

Men in SGR fear the protagonists. "It's not a new phenom-enon to Saudi," Fahad said. "Men are made to fear women and any type of advancements that come from them—they feel that it's somehow going to take power away from them."

The second "season" of SGR will be an action-adventure mobile game with seven playable characters. The levels in the game will be short—two minutes at most. Fahad quickly showed us one of the levels while we were sitting in the upstairs drawing room in Kensington. It was the iPad version of the game. A slender, raven-haired protagonist in a long cloak jumped gracefully between platforms in an underground level filled with glistening pipes and dangerous drops. She was wielding a sword.

At first, the idea that a video game like SGR can help shift ingrained cultural biases seems naïve, but Egyptian-Dutch game developer Rami Ismail, who has spoken at length about cultural stereotyping in games, particularly Western games' portrayal of Arab and Muslim characters, says that the problem is largely a result of ignorance. "To Western developers, the Middle East is as much a fictional place as Middle Earth, and the inhabitants as real as the Orcs," he told us recently.

Ismail argues that games have a better shot than other media at turning things around—especially in a region where the predominant demographic is under 30. Some games have tried: The Cat and the Coup, for example, is a 2011 puzzle game about the life of Iran's celebrated former prime minister Mohammed Mossadegh, who was overthrown by the CIA and MI6 in 1953 and forced to spend the rest of his days under house arrest. The game was released through the digital distribution platform Steam and short-listed for several game industry awards, including the news game category at the 2011 Games for Change festival. But few games made in or about the Middle East have the means and financial backing to profit from the same distribution channels as games like Call of Duty.

Alston is adamant that she is not seeking validation from the West. "We want it to be a hit in the Middle East first. We want people in the West to play it, of course, but we're not in search for a stamp of approval. We want to empower our own community first."

In an industry that barely existed ten years ago, NA3M has survived—and thrived—for three years running. Fahad likes to tell the story of a young Jordanian employee who used to come into the office dressed all in black, and who would rarely speak to her colleagues.

"Now, she wears bright ensembles and heels, and has spirited discussions with her colleagues about culture and religion," he told us. Fahad views this as a small victory—even if the ongoing refrain in the West is that more needs to be done for women's rights throughout the Middle East. "More needs to be done everywhere," Fahad continued. "Until women are treated equally everywhere, there's no moral ground for comparison anywhere. We all have work to do.

"Until we change global perceptions about Arabs and our region in general, every moment of progress is going to be questioned and scrutinized." He paused, then added: "It's important to remember that this is modernization, not Westernization."

5.

Nine Minutes of Pregnancy

(THE STORY OF THE HALF THE SKY MOVEMENT)

In the summer of 2012, Games for Change co-president Michelle Byrd traveled to Nairobi, Kenya, with a bag full of mobile phones. Each phone was preloaded with a game called 9 Minutes. The game, co-developed by Games for Change, was created to teach pregnant women in developing countries about nutrition and best practices during pregnancy, like how much sleep to get and when it's necessary to visit a doctor. It plays like an arcade game, in which the player must identify and collect "positive" icons related to diet, health, and behavior,[1] and ignore "negative" ones. (For example, tomatoes and fruit count as positive, while coffee and wine are negative.) There are nine levels in total, no longer than a minute each, to represent the nine months of pregnancy. At the end of each level, a text pop-up informs players what they got right and wrong and makes suggestions regarding checkups, HIV testing, and other health-related matters.

In Kenya, Byrd visited schools, community centers, youth leadership organizations, and medical clinics, showing the game to as many people as possible—both women and men.[2] More than 65 percent of Kenya's 40 million people own mobile phones; in Kibera, Africa's largest slum, home to some one million people, more than 75 percent of inhabitants have access to mobile devices. Maternal mortality is especially prevalent in Kibera, where one in 26 women dies in childbirth. At one of the slum's busy clinics, Byrd met with the director and a handful of her patients, all young women who watched patiently as Byrd explained how the game worked.

"A lot of women in Nairobi don't believe there's any real need to start pregnancy visits until they're showing," the director of the clinic told Byrd. "Some think it's okay to just deliver at home."

Byrd showed one young woman the game. "So, should you eat a tomato while you're pregnant?" Byrd asked the woman. The woman hesitated, and then nodded slowly. "There's reticence for these women to talk openly about their bodies," Byrd said recently. "The game was like an icebreaker—a small window into what each woman was doing day-to-day, what she was eating, how much sleep she was getting, and so on."

A reporter from Kenyan TV showed up to film a segment about the women playing 9 Minutes.[3] After interviewing some of those who had played the game, she turned to the camera and noted that while 9 Minutes seemed to offer plenty of health tips, many of the women who turned up to the clinic would be glad just to have something to do while waiting in line.

THE GAME 9 MINUTES was one of four games—one Facebook game and three mobile games—developed in partnership with the Half the Sky Movement, spearheaded by journalist and author Sheryl WuDunn and her husband, *New York Times* columnist Nicholas Kristof.

The story begins with the publication of Kristof and Wu-Dunn's book *Half the Sky: Turning Oppression into Opportunity for Women Worldwide*, in 2009. In the book, Kristof and WuDunn describe the oppression of women around the world as the "paramount moral challenge" of our time.[4] WuDunn has written and lectured extensively on the economic, political, and social status of women in the developing world and in the United States. Kristof is a celebrated reporter whose column often focuses on international humanitarian issues. Together, the couple covered the 1989 Tiananmen Square massacre in China for the *Times*; a year later, they won the Pulitzer Prize for journalism—the first married couple to do so. (Kristof won a second Pulitzer in 2006 for his coverage of the genocide in Darfur.)

But in *Half the Sky*, Kristof and WuDunn do more than report. Chapter by chapter, they recount their personal experiences traveling through Asia and Africa, meeting girls and women struggling against a system that is determined to favor their oppressors: women who are beaten, raped, and sold into slavery; who are stoned or burned to death if they are considered to have brought shame upon their families; or whose faces and bodies are disfigured by acid.

The stories are tragic but not without hope. Many of the women Kristof and WuDunn profile are survivors. A Cambodian teenager, Srey Rath, who was sold into sex slavery, escaped from her brothel and went on to become a successful businesswoman. Mamitu, an Ethiopian woman who suffered an obstetric fistula as a result of a prolonged, obstructed labor in her first pregnancy, hung around the surgeon who helped treat her and eventually learned to do fistula operations herself. A Pakistani girl, Mukhtar Mai, who was gang-raped, fought for her rights. Eventually, Pervez Musharraf, who was Pakistan's president at the time, directed that the government award her compensation. She used the money to open a school in her village.

Look at these women, WuDunn and Kristof say—look how they turned their narrative around to thrive and become leaders in their communities.

Now, imagine what else they could have done if they'd only had a little help. In their introduction, the authors describe the event that motivated them to write the book. Tiananmen Square was the human rights story of 1989, but in 1990, Kristof and WuDunn stumbled upon another human rights violation, one few people knew about: according to an obscure demographic study, 39,000 baby girls died annually in China because their parents didn't provide them with the same medical attention that boys in the family received. A Chinese family-planning official described the situation to Kristof and WuDunn this way: "If a boy gets sick, the parents may send him to the hospital at once. But if a girl gets sick, the parents may say to themselves, 'Well, let's see how she is tomorrow.'"

Where were the news reports about this? "Those Chinese girls never received a column inch of news coverage, and we began to wonder if our journalistic priorities were skewed," Kristof and WuDunn wrote. They began to see similar patterns in South Asia and the Middle East. In India, they discovered that bride burning, or dowry killings, occur roughly once every two hours, a horrific practice that is common when a husband's family believes they have not received enough money as part of the wedding dowry and the bride's family is unable to pay more. In Pakistan, they found that some 5,000 women and girls had been doused in kerosene and set alight by family members in the preceding nine years. According to the United States Agency for International Development (USAID), which is responsible for foreign aid, 62 million girls around the world are not in school, and an estimated 100 million will drop out before completing primary school. Globally, one in seven girls marries before turning 15, and one in three women experience gender-based violence.[5]

"When a prominent dissident was arrested in China, we would write a front-page article; when 100,000 girls were routinely kidnapped and trafficked into brothels, we didn't even consider it news," Kristof and WuDunn wrote. "Partly that is because we journalists tend to be good at covering events that happen on a particular day, but we slip at covering events that happen every day—such as the quotidian cruelties inflicted on women and girls. We journalists weren't the only ones who dropped the ball on this subject: less than one percent of US foreign aid is specifically targeted to women and girls." (This figure has improved significantly since then: the majority of foreign aid now goes to health pro-grams, particularly HIV/AIDS and maternal and child health initiatives.)[6]

Critics loved the book, praising its scope and message. It hit #1 on the *New York Times* bestsellers list for nonfiction books, and found a sizable international readership. Celebrities liked it too. "These stories show us the power and resilience of women who would have every reason to give up, but never do," Angelina Jolie wrote of *Half the Sky*. Here's George Clooney: "I think it's impossible to stand by and do nothing after reading *Half the Sky*." Then Oprah Winfrey took up the cause,[7] and the Half the Sky Movement, as it came to be known, was born.

THE MOST ORDINARY THING you can say about Kristof is that he grew up on a farm in Oregon. He graduated from Harvard, won a Rhodes Scholarship to study law at Oxford, and then traveled to Egypt to study Arabic and to Taipei to study Chinese. Even adolescent rites of passage, like backpacking through Asia, had a certain spin in Kristof's life: instead of working in bars or coffee shops to cover his expenses, a young Kristof wrote articles about the injustices he was witnessing in the places he traveled.

On a recent Thursday morning, we joined Kristof in his airy corner office on the thirteenth floor of the *New York Times* building in Manhattan. "I'm going to sit facing the door," he said. "So I can see any interruptions coming." Kristof is quiet and thoughtful, if somewhat scatterbrained. His assistant, who works in a cubicle directly outside his office door, manages his appointments and day-to-day schedule. He listens to questions patiently and answers only when he's ready. "The problem with books," he said, reclining in his chair, "is that they preach to the choir. We wanted to expand the choir."

In 2012, a two-part documentary based on Kristof and WuDunn's book aired on PBS[8] and was watched by over five million people. The four-hour series followed Kristof around ten countries—Cambodia, Kenya, India, Sierra Leone, Somaliland, Vietnam, Afghanistan, Pakistan, Liberia, and the United States—as he visited and talked to women whose lives have been impacted by sex trafficking, forced prostitution, child labor, maternal mortality, violence, and financial and educational hardship. The documentary was basically the book in visual form, except that this time, the authors weren't alone: they were joined by a handful of female celebrity advocates, including America Ferrera, Diane Lane, Eva Mendes, Meg Ryan, Gabrielle Union, and Olivia Wilde.

The documentary, like the book, was a success. But it had come very close to being something completely different.

While Kristof was filming *Reporter,* a 2009 documentary that followed him to eastern Congo with the two winners of his annual Win a Trip contest—in which readers enter for the chance to accompany Kristof on one of his reporting trips—Mikaela Beardsley, the producer behind the documentary, had optioned the rights to *Half the Sky,* which Kristof and WuDunn were halfway through writing, with the intention of turning it into a series. But Beardsley ran into trouble trying to get it off the ground. Part of the problem was the original concept. Beardsley wanted to create a series of fictionalized shorts directed by different actresses who had shown support for the humanitarian efforts described in *Half the Sky.* (One source close to the project, who wished to remain anonymous, said, "Actresses act. Who knows if they can direct? It was risky from the beginning.")

Beardsley did end up filming two shorts, one directed by Marisa Tomei, and the other by Lucy Liu. Each short presented a dramatized version of a story from *Half the Sky*. Ultimately however, it was hard to find funding, and conversations with the Corporation for Public Broadcasting (CPB)—a nonprofit that invests the government's public broadcasting budget in public radio, television, and online services—eventually stalled.

But Pat Harrison, CPB's president and CEO, was intrigued. As the chairman of the Leadership Council of Women and Girls Lead, a public media initiative focused on educating and connecting women around the world, Harrison wanted to know more about *Half the Sky*. She told Kristof, WuDunn, and Beardsley that she wanted to ultimately fund the project, but not in its current form. She urged Beardsley to talk to someone else in the industry who might be able to pull the whole thing together.

Enter Maro Chermayeff. An award-winning filmmaker and producer based in New York, Chermayeff knew immediately what she wanted: a documentary that, like the book, would follow Kristof in the field. The celebrities could still be in it: they'd be good for attracting audiences to the cause. The section of the population unlikely to be interested in reading a book about female oppression might be more interested in watching a documentary on the same subject if Hollywood celebrities were involved.

Chermayeff and Kristof hit it off immediately. "We are polar opposites of the same person," Chermayeff said. "He has a huge sense of humor but he doesn't know it." We were sitting in her sunlit office at Show of Force, her production company, in New York's TriBeCa neighborhood. Her window ledge served as an awards cabinet: an Emmy seemed to sparkle brightest in the morning sun.

Chermayeff and Kristof began work on the documentary in late 2010. The format was easy: each episode would feature Kristof, a celebrity, and a country. Chermayeff and her team worked with local humanitarian organizations and NGOs in each country, plotting the locations and the arcs of the stories and finding women who could be interviewed on camera. A crew was assembled: camera people, translators, and vehicles. Then it was time to pick the celebrities. Chermayeff wanted actresses who'd already engaged in one way or another with the issues explored in *Half the Sky*. "We didn't go for, I don't know, Katy Perry, or something," she said. Kristof had little input—he didn't know who most of the actresses were anyway. According to Chermayeff, he doesn't watch television and rarely watches movies. (This is all the more amusing given that when you Google Kristof, most of the top results are photos of celebrities posing with him at various charity events.) Kristof was once brought into a room to meet Angelina Jolie; when he walked in, he saw three women sitting on a couch. He did not know which one was Jolie. "She eventually recognized my distress and stood up to greet me," Kristof confessed.

The actresses, on the other hand, knew who Kristof was. "Almost everybody we called up said yes almost as soon as we asked them," Chermayeff said. Olivia Wilde went with Kristof to Kenya, where they met a woman who had run away from her abusive husband and started a women's-only village, where she taught other women about financial and sexual empowerment. In Cambodia,

Meg Ryan talked to girls who'd spent most of their lives in locked rooms, forced to have sex with adult men ten to 15 times a day. Eva Mendes accompanied Kristof to Sierra Leone, where rape and sexual assault are part of the weaponry of war.

Despite the exhaustive work that went into each shoot, things didn't always go according to plan. Once, the team stumbled upon a young rape victim in Sierra Leone who was trying to get her case heard by a court. Kristof tracked down her alleged rapist himself and simply called him on the phone while the camera was running. "Suddenly, we were directly involved," Chermayeff said. The man was arrested and taken to a local prison. The documentary team followed. Chermayeff wanted Kristof to interview the man, but they needed a release form. So Chermayeff went inside to try to persuade him to speak on camera. "Cut to Maro in a dirty Sierra Leone prison surrounded by nine guys accused of rape," Chermayeff recalled.

On the same shoot, while driving along a dirt road, the team came across a burned-out vehicle a few feet from the road, in a field. They stopped, and Kristof and Chermayeff got out to investigate. As they approached, Chermayeff noticed that the rocks on the ground had been painted different colors—some blue, others red. "What are all these rocks? Why are they painted?" she asked Kristof. Kristof replied, without a hint of panic, "I think we might be in a minefield." Chermayeff freaked out. "So does red mean mine? Or does blue mean mine?" Kristof shrugged. "I don't remember. Let's just go out the way we came."

There were also challenges imposed by what the team could and could not show on television. Female genital mutilation, for example. How do you show the horror on film? "We had a video of a girl being cut, but it was just inappropriate to show on television," Kristof recalled. "So what we did instead was film Diane Lane watching the video—and her face, as she saw this girl get hacked apart, captured the horror of it in a way that was incredibly powerful." Not everyone was on board with the celebrity angle. "By making himself the central, solo, and dominant hero in the narrative of fighting gender inequality, Kristof tends to undercut the very goals of women's empowerment that he espouses so vociferously," wrote Sunil Bhatia in the *Feminist Wire* in 2013.[9] The celebrated novelist and historian Teju Cole expressed a similar sentiment in 2012 when he tweeted: "From Sachs to Kristof to Invisible Children to TED, the fastest growth industry in the US is the White Savior Industrial Complex." In a follow-up piece for the *Atlantic*,[10] Cole pointed to the principle of "first, do no harm," meaning in this case that those who are being helped should be consulted over those issues that pertain to them and their livelihood. He conceded: "I do not accuse Kristof of racism nor do I believe he is in any way racist. I have no doubt that he has a good heart."

Kristof is used to this kind of criticism. "The problem is not that white Americans are overeager to help people of color," he said in his office. "The problem is that white people are willing to let people of color die around the world . . . we're willing to save the lives of white Bosnians but not black Rwandans."

KRISTOF IS THE FIRST to admit that he doesn't know anything about video games, but his day job at the *Times* had given him plenty of experience with finding ways to reach new audiences. That is why he is so active on social media and why he blogs frequently.

Kristof remembers that during the filming of the *Half the Sky* documentary, a lot of people talked about a Facebook game called FarmVille. "Everyone was playing it at that point. Everyone except me, of course. But I thought, 'Oh boy, if there could just be something similar about Half the Sky, that would be great.' Because there's no barrier to entry, is there? You don't have to already care about women around the world to play a game. All I knew was that video games were drawing a ton of eyeballs, and that was what we wanted." Anyone not likely to be interested in either the book or the documentary might be reached through a video game.

So Kristof asked Games for Change for help. By mid-2010, Asi Burak and Michelle Byrd had joined the organization as co-presidents and were immediately tasked with seeking funding for a proposed Half the Sky Facebook game. "We were piggybacking on the whole machine that had raised $10 million altogether for the [cross-platform] project, money from Intel and IKEA and Goldman Sachs, and the Gates Foundation," Asi recalled. On one hand, Games for Change, or G4C, would benefit from being associated with the Half the Sky Movement; on the other hand, the games effort was at the bottom of the investors' list. There were no celebrities involved, and while Facebook games were on the rise, few people understood why they'd become so popular. Anyway, this wasn't FarmVille—it had to be a serious, socially impactful game that would marry entertainment with measurable real-world action.

The proposed idea was for an adventure game that would raise awareness of the struggle of women and girls around the world while also allowing players to donate money to various causes. Players would take on the role of a young Indian girl, Radhika, who faced daily struggles related to poverty, education, and health. Simply playing the game was free, but players could make faster progress by donating virtual goods to help Radhika.

At the same time, the game also allowed for the equivalent of real-world donations to various nonprofits like Room to Read and the Fistula Foundation. Playing the game unlocked donations from companies such as Johnson & Johnson and Pearson Education, with each contributing $250,000 to the effort, targeted at free surgeries and books, respectively. The initial hope was that the game would reach up to five million players, with around 5 percent making real-world donations.

The goal was to release the game at the same time as the PBS documentary, to maximize impact. But finding funding proved difficult. At one point, Chermayeff, who was coordinating behind-the-scenes, asked Games for Change what the holdup was. Asi considered giving up. "We were desperate," he recalled. Then, in late 2011, a breakthrough came: G4C was asked to appear alongside Kristof at Mashable's Social Good summit. The actress Geena Davis was there too. The panel moderator was Aaron Sherinian, the chief communications and marketing officer at the UN Foundation. "He called me after the panel and said, 'I'll convince the UN Foundation to give you $100,000,'" Asi recalled. And he did.

G4C initially believed the game would cost around $500,000 to make, not including marketing. But as *Half the Sky* became more popular, the budget and scope of the game ballooned. Asi had already put out a call for proposals from video game companies that could take on the task. One day, a studio from Quebec called Frima sent in its proposal. "I gave it one look and called Nick," Asi said. "I said, we're at the breaking point, and we have this amazing proposal. We need to move on it—now." Asi was struck by the sensibility with which Frima had approached the proposal. (More on this later.) All G4C had was the UN Foundation's $100,000. If they wanted to move forward, they'd need much more than that. Asi reminded Kristof of something they'd spoken about at the beginning: if push came to shove, Asi remembered Kristof saying, the Ford Foundation might be able to help out.

Kristof agreed and arranged a phone call with the then-president of the Ford Foundation, Luis Antonio Ubinas. (He left in 2013.) Chermayeff joined Kristof and Asi on the call. "It was one of the most important calls of my life," Asi said. He was seated in his office, at G4C's headquarters in New York. It was morning, but he hadn't eaten breakfast. Part of the problem was that unlike other nonprofit leaders, Ubinas knew the games industry—he'd been a board director at Electronic Arts, one of the largest gaming publishers. Perhaps because he was so knowledgeable, Ubinas was also skeptical. Ubinas asked how much money G4C needed to make the Half the Sky Facebook game; Asi replied that it would take an additional $400,000. "We wanted to ask for something reasonable that would push us to a place where we could start." When Asi revealed G4C hoped to attract between one and five million players, Ubinas replied, "You're joking." He knew the numbers of commercial Facebook games, and he didn't think it would happen. "It was like, [Ubinas] was trying to convince Nick that I was selling him dreams that were never going to come to fruition," Asi recalled. Chermayeff and Kristof later joked that Asi had been kicking himself under the table.

The next day, Asi called Kristof to apologize. He also sent Ubinas a follow-up email detailing why G4C was the right organization to take this on. He included some history about the organization: what they'd done, how they'd done it, and accolades from the industry for their work. He received a two-line reply from Darren Walker, Ubinas's deputy, who is now the president of the Ford Foundation. "We'll get back to you, this is very helpful," Walker wrote. Four days later, Kristof called Asi and Byrd. The Ford Foundation would contribute $400,000 for the Facebook game. "Ford didn't say they were doing it for Nick, but that was the feeling. The money was in our account in the following week," Asi said.

OVER IN QUEBEC CITY at Frima Studio, Gabriel Lefebvre was finally finding a use for his background in anthropology. After studying creative writing in college, the game designer switched to history and comparative religion before finally focusing on the anthropology of myths in the Western world. Game design had been just a hobby for him at first, but after nearing the end of his PhD and finding no open positions in academia, Lefebvre landed a job at Sarbakan, a small Quebec-based game studio. He moved to Frima a few years later as a design director.

One day, he was called into a meeting to help brainstorm ideas for a project called Half the Sky. He was stumped. "Themes like economic empowerment and access to health care are easy enough to match with game mechanics, but when you're adding violence and sexual abuse, it becomes mind-boggling. We enter the realm where 'fun' needs to build on experiences that may not be fun intrinsically."

What's more, this was to be a game on Facebook, at the time the biggest platform for gaming. Lefebvre knew that successful Facebook games relied on daily engagement with not-too-heavy game content. "You play the games during your coffee breaks, to escape your job for a moment. How could we reconcile the requirement of the platform's public to the complex, nuanced, and serious nature of the content we wanted to deliver them?"

There was a lot of debate among the Frima team about what to include and how. For one thing, the game had to tell a story players would fall in love with and stay attached to over a long period of time, while still portraying real-world situations in all their subtlety and routine. How could the game be both palatable and impactful without feeling like exploitation?

Lefebvre became personally invested in the project. He read Kristof and WuDunn's book. Raised by a single mother who ran her own kindergarten, and now raising a daughter of his own, Lefebvre felt a responsibility to use his abilities to bring about change—or, at the very least, raise awareness. As soon as Frima's proposal was accepted and the Ford Foundation's grant came through, Lefebvre pushed aside his other projects and concentrated solely on the Half the Sky game.

Lefebvre knew the pitfalls of immersive storytelling—it's expensive, for starters, and mid-production changes in story can cause trouble. To alleviate risks, Lefebvre and the team decided to present the stories in small, self-enclosed segments, based on dialogue and simple action. Any change would thus be limited to that segment and affect only the writing. The team then created tools to modify the story elements.

The game begins with Radhika asking players to help her make a decision. How can she make enough money to afford a doctor's visit for her sick daughter? There are a few options. Players can ask Radhika's husband for help, but all he will say is that he doesn't understand why the family resources should be spent on their daughter and not their son. The progressive choice is harvesting and selling mangoes, which sets Radhika on a long path to independence: she ends up helping her own family, then her community, and finally becomes a role model who speaks in front of the UN.

Not all aspects of the game are as uplifting; players are sometimes faced with tough choices, and there are grim elements—the final level of the game deals with sex trafficking in the United States, for example. Overall, however, the game is optimistic, an aspect Asi had to defend on several occasions to various partners and investors, including Zynga, which provided support, and the National Endowment for the Arts. "Yes, it's a cartoony game, but not because we're ignoring the seriousness of some of these themes but because we wanted to make it engaging and similar to other playful experiences on Facebook," Asi said recently. An early criticism from G4C's investment partners concerned the mango-harvesting scene—that it could be perceived as suggesting that everything has a simple fix. "You can't go too deep on the content, otherwise no one will play it," Asi said. "The mango activity is fun, empowering, and breaks the gloom—and it shows players that they can make progress right away. This is how you deal with serious issues in an interactive medium."

Lefebvre agrees. "The game necessarily sacrificed a portion of realism, and this means accepting shortcuts and not-quite-exact depictions of reality. My own daughter played the game over several months and even brought some of her friends to it. When she first saw the Afghan girl character with the acid scars on her face, it prompted a discussion."

AT SOME POINT DURING the development of the game, it became clear that having Half the Sky on Facebook wouldn't be enough. Millions of users in developing countries rely solely on low-cost handsets for their daily communication and information. There are some 3.6 billion mobile phone users in the world, and more than 60 percent of them are in developing countries.[11] But they don't necessarily have Facebook. It made sense to develop a mobile game or games as part of the Half the Sky Movement.

But what would those games be about? Who would they target? How complex could they be, given the technological restrictions in many developing countries?

While the mobile phone penetration in developing countries was growing at that time, many of the phones themselves could only support games no larger than 200KB. It was all very well to imagine that young women and girls in rural communities could pick up mobile phones and simply play games aimed at improving their health and well-being, but everyone knew it wasn't that simple.

In 2011, Asi joined up with Alan Gershenfeld, the former chairman of G4C, who continues to serve on its advisory board. Gershenfeld and his company, E-Line Media, were instrumental in conceiving the Half the Sky mobile games and later helped with their distribution in India and Kenya. Gershenfeld had contacts in India—twin brothers who had formed a mobile video game studio called ZMQ. Their goal was to create social-impact games for India's underserved communities. They'd had a national hit in 2005—one of their games about HIV prevention had become so popular that the government had incorporated it into a public campaign. Gershenfeld contacted ZMQ and asked them about Half the Sky. Could this work on mobile? Sure, they said. Why don't you come down here and we can show you where the games might have the most impact.

At first, Asi said, Kristof didn't show much interest in the Half the Sky mobile games. But Asi thought he had a way to convince him. At the time, G4C was in talks with USAID about another gaming project. Asi wondered if they'd be receptive to hearing a pitch on the Half the Sky mobile games. USAID came on board almost immediately, giving the project some $300,000. (An extra $2.5 million came later, in 2013, after the launch of both the Facebook and mobile games. This grant was intended to help in the distribution and evaluation of the documentary and games in countries including India and Kenya.) Asi found another game development studio, Mudlark, based in the UK, which agreed to take on the challenge of making a mobile game under 200KB whose primary goal was to change the lives of young women in developing countries. In India, ZMQ would work to set up meetings with different NGOs and organize trips to rural communities, where Asi and Gershenfeld could better grasp the issues facing young girls and women. The mobile games would have to address one of the issues covered in Half the Sky, that much was clear.

But which: health? Sex trafficking? Education? "We didn't want at any cost to be the white crusaders coming in and fixing things," Asi recalled. "We wanted to understand from the people we were meeting what problems we needed to address with these games."

Asi, Gershenfeld, and a representative from Mudlark landed in Delhi. The first meeting was with ZMQ, at their offices in a suburb of the city, part of a shabby-looking low-rise encircled by a security gate and a high-wire fence. "People used to break in and steal their computers, so they added some security," Asi said. The office itself was a couple of rooms with desks, chairs, and computer terminals. The walls were mostly bare except for some promotional posters advertising ZMQ's HIV game.

"At that first meeting, we talked about accessibility. We were going to have players who had never played a game before." The team also learned that in poorer rural communities in India, a mobile phone is a necessity, not a luxury. In many homes there are no landlines, and there's usually only one mobile phone per family. The children are able to use it only for an hour or so a day, usually to play games. Many parents Asi spoke to told him they wished there was more educational content available on the phones.

The next day, the twins took the team to a poor neighborhood in the suburbs of Delhi that was a busy area for sex trafficking. ZMQ had arranged an interview with one of the area's big bosses—a frail, old man with hardly any teeth who sold his own daughters and everyone else's in the neighborhood, too. He owned a club farther down the road that provided nightly entertainment in the form of lounge acts but was used mostly as a brothel. "Like a community center, but for sex trafficking," Asi recalled.

Asi and the team were invited into the man's home. They sat

down to tea and were soon joined by the man's daughters and granddaughters. Everyone was smiling. Some of the younger girls were pregnant. At one point, the man brought out a basket and showed his visitors what was inside: a huge, white snake that looked frail and sickly. "We all jumped back, horrified." The man explained that he'd been a snake charmer. Snake charming was the family business when he was growing up. But when international animal rights organizations shut down the snake-charming trade in India, his family members were suddenly out of work. So they turned to sex trafficking. "NGOs basically solved one problem and created another," Asi said.

The next day, Asi and the team met with an aid organization, from which they learned that India has an extraordinarily high rate of unsuccessful pregnancies, usually resulting in miscarriage, newborn death, and even the deaths of mothers. According to US-AID, more than 287,000 women die each year from pregnancy- and childbirth-related complications, 99 percent of them in developing countries. Most of this is due to a lack of information, particularly in rural communities. Young women and girls have no money to go to doctors or to buy vitamins or supplements; there's no information about nutritional guidelines or the inadvisability of, for example, lifting heavy objects when pregnant. Asi and Gershenfeld looked at each other. This could be it. They asked other organizations they met with: is pregnancy the major issue here? Almost everyone they spoke with said yes.

For the rest of the week, the team sat in front of a whiteboard in ZMQ's office and spitballed ideas. They came up with a game centered on pregnancy, and 9 Minutes was born. The brainstorming session also turned up a second game, called Worm Attack.

Kristof had written a lot about intestinal worms, a big concern in developing countries because of the prevalence of unwashed hands and bare feet. Young women are even more at risk due to a lack of proper hygiene during menstruation. NGOs usually give out free pills that both prevent the infection and fight the condition if hosts are already infected. So if a pill can be so effective and simple, why not make a game that will show kids how worms are attacking their bodies, using the pills as weapons against infection? In the end, three games were developed for communities in India and Kenya. The third game, called Family Choices, highlights the value of girls and their roles in the larger family structure. This one was more ambitious than 9 Minutes and Worm Attack: it plays out almost like a soap opera, with a choose-your-own-adventure structure. Players must decide whether Anu (in India) or Mercy (in Kenya) can ultimately achieve her dream of becoming a financially independent nurse. The focus is on continuing education for young women, as opposed to early marriage, while understanding the trade-offs and consequences.

The games launched in November 2012. They were each under 200KB and, except for a one-time download, did not require an internet connection. They could be played in English, Hindi, and Kiswahili and procured through in-country mobile phone app stores, including Nokia, Safaricom, GetJar, and Appia. The point of Byrd's trip to Kenya was to assess the games' impact.

"We had info on what kind of phones people were using, but the prevalence of phones and how connected people were just blew us away," Byrd said later. "I was also surprised at how quickly the young people understood the language of games. They all had access to their parents' phones and knew immediately how to play the games."

The Half the Sky Facebook game was released in March 2013. Zynga's involvement attracted press, and players soon followed. And yet, according to Asi, the most successful marketing tools for the game—i.e., what actually got people to play it—were paid Facebook ads and Zynga's own banners and plugs on their other games. This was somewhat of a surprise, given the amount of hype and celebrity endorsement surrounding the entire Half the Sky Movement. "The bottom line seemed to be that it's easy to bring a random Facebook player who does not care about social issues to play another Facebook game with a purpose, but it's not so easy to convince someone who cares about a social issue to go on Facebook and play a game about it."

TO DATE, THE HALF the Sky Movement has raised over $7 million, which it has donated to organizations focused on helping women and girls in developing countries. More than 1.3 million people have registered and played the Facebook game.[12]

During the documentary broadcast, messaging from brands, organizations, and individuals related to the Half the Sky Movement generated one billion impressions across the three days of social media activity (October 1–3, 2012). The hashtag #HalftheSky trended domestically and internationally on Twitter on both October 1 and 2. (Tweets of support from celebrities, including Oprah Winfrey, Ben Affleck, Ashton Kutcher, Jessica Alba, and Russell Simmons, helped significantly.) There were also hundreds of smaller civilian efforts, people who were inspired by the movement to act on their own. While Olivia Wilde was recording the audio book version of *A Path Appears*, the follow-up to *Half the Sky*, which later inspired a documentary of the same name, the audio engineer working that day, Kevin Thomsen, was so moved by what he was hearing that he decided to start his own initiative, going around the world to record kids' stories for young American listeners. (Both of Thomsen's daughters are adopted—one from the Republic of Georgia, the other from Ethiopia.) The project, known as Red Trunk, is still being developed. Some time later, Kristof received a note from an inmate at a state women's prison in Connecticut who had read *Half the Sky* to the other inmates and started her own fund-raising project.

Players of the Facebook game gave more than $500,000 in total donations, including more than $200,000 for fistula surgeries and some 250,000 free books. The Half the Sky Facebook game became the number-nine emerging game on Facebook within two weeks of its release, side by side with commercial entertainment titles. Given that there are more than two thousand games on Facebook at any given time, this was quite an achievement.

Mostly, the game appealed to female players—who, in fact, made up 80 percent of all players. (This is also in line with research that suggests that the average player on Facebook is female and 39 years old.) The original aim of the game was to inspire people to spend between 15 and 30 minutes playing the game; the average play session ended up being 14 minutes. The game's launch was also supported by events in Los Angeles, New York, Washington, DC, and Quebec City, where many of the celebrities involved in the documentary showed up to support the cause.

In December 2012, USAID conducted an impact evaluation

of 9 Minutes.[13] The report details the results of a study conducted in India, in which 608 women and 308 men participated. The study, which involved focus group discussions, play sessions, and pre- and postgame reporting, included married women aged 18–44, who were pregnant or intended to become pregnant within the next year, and husbands of women of reproductive age who were pregnant or intended to conceive within the next year. The aim of the study was to measure how familiar both men and women were with safe pregnancy practices prior to game exposure, and whether playing the game shifted their perceptions, knowledge, and intentions. The study randomly assigned participants to two groups: one group was only given 9 Minutes to play, while the other group played the game, watched a related video, and participated in a brief, facilitated small-group discussion. Those activities were conducted to measure how successful the game alone could be in changing attitudes, as opposed to the game in combination with other media.

Participants' knowledge and understanding of beneficial pregnancy activities rose significantly after they played the game. For example, before playing the game, very few participants recognized the value during pregnancy of activities such as drinking water, resting, and saving money. (Those practices contrasted with "eat nutritious foods," which was the one activity almost all participants identified, both pre- and postgame, as being important.) Most importantly, participants showed increased self-efficacy and intention to act on matters such as getting antenatal checkups, testing for HIV, and taking vitamins regularly.

However, the evaluation also acknowledged that while the game had had a positive impact, it was hard to know whether the effects would continue outside a controlled environment. "The bottom line is, when things are not about a basic necessity, like water or food or safety, you do need the intervention of NGOs," Chermayeff said. "The idea that you live in a village and your husband is beating you and you're going to sit around playing a game, well . . ."

Looking back, Chermayeff says the cross-platform project was ultimately successful in its goal of reaching a wide audience. Byrd said her key takeaway was that the timing could have been better—she still wonders what would have happened if the games, both Facebook and mobile, had launched at the same time as the documentary. "It would have been interesting to have seen how much more reach we could have had if we'd been able to piggyback off that momentum."

Chermayeff says she always knew it would be hard to keep audiences and stakeholders consistently interested over a period of some years. "We rode a wave and drove attention to our project, and we did it at the right time. But if you come a little too late or too early, it's much harder. And then, once you're done, people are no longer interested. They say, 'Oh, we've already talked about women and girls. This problem is still happening? I thought we'd fixed it.'"

With the benefit of hindsight, Kristof says he might have pursued a randomized controlled trial of the mobile games to test whether they did, in fact, have an impact on behavior long-term. (Randomized controlled trials, which are extremely expensive, follow participants consistently over a period of time—sometime years—gathering evidence about whether the sought-after effect is actually taking place.) Kristof says that while the USAID impact study showed that 9 Minutes had had a positive impact on attitudes, it couldn't provide clear metrics on whether the game had helped save lives. He also feels that he might have made both the book and documentary more uplifting, to convey the idea that while the situation is bleak, there is certainly hope. "Both the book and documentary scared people, I think—especially men. It seemed depressing and tough. So many people told me they started it and they gave up because it was simply too bleak. For us, we had just been immersed in this world for so long that we maybe we got a little bit numb to how hard these stories were to take."

Ultimately, Half the Sky changed how Show of Force approaches its new projects: the company is now working on a film about the eradication of polio and on another project having to do with refugees. "We are on this Earth only once, and people that are really well off and educated have to use what they have to try and make things better for other people," Chermayeff said. "It's fun to play Fruit Ninja when you're stuck in an airport—but it doesn't mean anything. What Nick will always be remembered for is that he did not quit. He kept going. He picked his beat, and he just. Kept. Going. He never stopped speaking into his megaphone."

PART III

FROM THE LAB TO THE SCREEN

Games that Aim to Solve Long-standing Scientific and Medical Problems.

6.

A Lab of Hope

(THE STORY OF RE-MISSION)

On an overcast Thursday morning in late October 2015, a young nurse stood on a chair in the waiting room of the Lucile Packard Children's Hospital at Stanford University, California. She was hanging Halloween decorations from the ceiling. Cotton spiderwebs framed two large windows overlooking an interior courtyard. Shiny black witches' hats stood at attention on tiny, pastel-colored tables. Pumpkin-shaped string lights looped around furniture corners and light fixtures. On the wall, below the permanent posters of Marvel superheroes and Star Wars characters, someone had stuck a life-size laughing skeleton.

A four-year-old girl with wiry blonde hair sat patiently on the waiting room couch, a multicolored surgical mask over her mouth. Jacob Lore, a recreation therapist, walked in holding a large folder and two iPads. The girl waved him over. "Hello," she said, standing up to greet him and putting one of her tiny hands on his hairy forearm. "Hey Maya," Lore said, sitting down next to her and offering her one of the iPads. "Want to play a game?"

Maya reached for the iPad and, without another look at Lore, began playing a chaotic-looking first-person shooter game. A swarm of grotesque-looking creatures descended from the top and sides of the screen; Maya deftly tapped the screen in various places, deploying different powers to disperse them. "Wow, Maya, you're doing really great," Lore said encouragingly. Maya ignored him. "What level are you on?" Lore tried again. "Eight," she said, and kept playing. Lore looked amused. "Once they start playing, there's no getting anything more out of them."

Lore is a child life specialist in the hospital's oncology ward. His job is to help young patients—who range from infants to late-20-somethings—adjust to hospitalization. This means constantly talking to patients about their diagnoses and treatment in a language they understand and creating an environment in which they feel safe. Lore likes to be present when younger patients like Maya undergo procedures such as getting IV drips put in; he'll often sit beside the children, asking them questions or showing them pictures or videos to distract them. The hospital's playroom—a brightly lit classroom space with toys, an art corner, a small kitchen, and a recreation room with televisions, video game consoles, and iPads—is a designated "safe space," meaning that doctors and nurses can come in and talk to the kids, but they cannot administer medicine or discuss treatment while inside. There's no talk of chemotherapy or checkups. "This is the one space they can come in to play without having to worry about someone coming in and saying or doing something that scares them," Lore said.

Before the iPad, Lore used to use a felt board to teach younger patients about things like chemotherapy and red and white blood cells. "But when things like iPads came along, I was having real trouble pulling them away from the screen to get them to look at a felt board," he said. In 2008, Lore was approached by a pediatric oncologist named Gary Dahl about a video game Dahl was helping to develop with the aim of informing young cancer patients about diagnosis and treatment. Specifically, he was working on a third-person shooter game called Re-Mission in which players pilot a microscopic robot named Roxxi through the bodies of fictional cancer patients, blasting away cancer cells. The game was slow to load and required several disks (the first version of the game was released in 2006), but Lore noticed that it essentially filled the same function as his felt board.

This was the game Maya was playing—at least, a newer version of it: shorter, quicker, and available on mobile devices and tablets. After another ten minutes, she logged out of the game and began running her small finger across the iPad screen, searching for something else. "What are you looking for?" Lore asked. "Angry Birds," she replied.

Lore sighed. "I'm always losing out to Angry Birds."

THE RE-MISSION GAMES WERE developed by HopeLab, a private nonprofit based in Redwood City, California. The company was founded in 2001 by Pam Omidyar and her husband, eBay founder Pierre Omidyar, to develop apps and games that improve the health of young people. The original Re-Mission was the lab's first game, made in the hope of encouraging young cancer patients to get more involved in their treatment by targeting specific psychological and behavioral outcomes, like motivation and self-efficacy. The grim environment of hospitals is not the only thing that can negatively impact a young person's ability to follow treatment: young patients have a hard time remembering to take their medicine, full stop. Habits and consistency are not their strong points. Pam Omidyar believed that helping young cancer patients visualize their bodies' responses to cancer might help motivate them to take more active roles in treatment. If they could just *see* how hard their bodies were working to repel the cancer, they'd be compelled to give the treatment their all.

In 1989, Pam Omidyar was a 22-year-old college graduate working as a research assistant in an immunology lab at Stanford University. She'd moved to California to be with her boyfriend, Pierre, who worked as a computer scientist. At the lab, her job was to grow different cancer cell lines so that the scientists could experiment on them. Sometimes, she assisted them, but her main job was to keep these cell cultures healthy. She spent her days staring down the barrel of a microscope, watching T-cells battle cancer cells.

"The idea was to find cell-specific markers, markers on the surface of cancer cells that cytotoxic T-cells could attack and kill in a very specific way," she said recently. At night, she and Pierre would play video games on their Sega Genesis. On the weekends, they'd go hiking or mountain biking.

The professor Omidyar worked for was a pediatric oncologist. Gradually, she began thinking about the kids whose cancer cell lines she was growing. "She could see this epic struggle taking place in the body of cancer patients, but she knew that cancer patients didn't feel like there was that much of an epic struggle,"

Steve Cole, HopeLab's vice president for research and development, said recently. We were sitting in a small, functional boardroom inside HopeLab's modest offices in Redwood City. Omidyar declined to attend—she preferred to communicate via email.

One day, Omidyar pictured her job in the form of a video game. She was the protagonist, tracking down cancer cells and attacking them with T-cells from a cool-looking laser gun. What if there was a game that utilized the same principles, but funneled them into something that really mattered, like a young patient's attitude toward fighting cancer? "She put those two things together and said, 'You know, if I can just show people cancer in the context of a game where they can battle it, then they are going to feel different about it,'" Cole said.

But video games aren't easy to make. Omidyar had no idea where to even begin looking for resources, and she eventually dropped the idea. Then, in 1995, eBay launched. Suddenly, Pam Omidyar had everything she needed.

On a sunny afternoon in the fall of 1999, Omidyar wandered into Stanford's development office and asked whom she could speak to about making a video game about cancer. She was shown to the door of Gary Dahl, the pediatric oncologist. Dahl immediately agreed to help and sent her to Pamela Kato, a Stanford health psychologist who shared Omidyar's love for video games. Kato was wrapping up postdoctoral work at Stanford in pediatric oncology. "I remember Gary coming to me and saying, 'There's this lady that made a lot of money in Silicon Valley and she wants to make something for kids with cancer,'" Kato said recently. "And I said, 'Okay, Gary, does she just want to give the kids a toy to make them feel better, or does she want to do this right?'"

Dahl told Kato to shut up and just go to the meeting. Kato was immediately taken with Omidyar's sincerity. "I've seen people waste money trying to help kids but they don't know what they're doing," she said. Dahl told Omidyar, "This may be the first time I'll be able to offer my kids a sense of control over their disease."

Initially, Kato worked as a consultant, writing proposals on what a game about cancer would look like, how it would be played, and whom it would benefit. She made contacts with video game designers and publishers. "The game wasn't intended to be clinical—it wasn't a new form of chemotherapy—but we believed it could help kids while they were going through this challenging part of their lives," Omidyar said. She didn't have an office; she and Kato met in coffee shops to give each other updates.

While Omidyar and Kato tried to come up with an actual methodology for developing the game, the hard-nosed Dahl warned them that the chances of success were slim: "There's not a lot of evidence that this is going to actually work," Cole remembered Dahl saying. "But I can tell you one thing: if your game can help my kids take their maintenance chemotherapy more reliably, or help them report symptoms at an earlier stage, that will make a huge difference." Dahl knew that too many young cancer patients die precisely as a result of failing to take those and other, similar, measures. If there was some way to help them remember to take their treatments, or motivate them to become more active and interested in their recovery, it could translate to an increase in survival rates.

That's when Kato called an old grad school friend—Cole. At the time, Cole was working as a professor of medicine at UCLA Cancer Center. "Steve, you're the only person I know who knows the backstory of the cells who can also speak the language of video games," she told him. "Help me turn this into a game." Cole agreed and came on board as a consultant.

The problem now was the game itself. Because its primary function was not entertainment, it would require different design and production parameters. No one seemed to know where to turn next. Omidyar reached out to major game developers "at the level of EA, Microsoft, and Nintendo"—she does not wish to name them. But no one was interested in taking things further. "In a business context, they couldn't justify the expense of creating a game for a small segment of the population," Omidyar said. "They didn't have the imagination to see how we could make a game about cancer cool and beautiful."

Omidyar and Kato knew they needed game designers, but it was difficult to find any willing to work alongside physicians. Physicians didn't understand the process of game design, and game designers didn't always want to include the clinically relevant information that Omidyar thought was important to achieve the game's purpose. "Game designers are fabulous at motivating kids to keep playing a game, and that's what we wanted—we wanted a game that kept kids playing by using the incentives and challenges that make games so engaging. But we also needed to put content into the game that would make it relevant to the cancer experience and help kids better understand their disease and how to fight it," Omidyar said.

Adherence to medication is crucial in cancer treatment. Ideally, the game would help young cancer patients to understand the correlation between the amount of chemo in their bodies and the ability of cancer cells to replicate the moment they stopped chemo.

Omidyar and Kato would sit around coffee shops in Mountain View trying to imagine what such a game would look like. They thought it would work best if set in the bloodstream. "What would it look like to actually navigate through the bloodstream in the heart? You'd have to wait for the valve to open, and you'd shoot through," Omidyar said. "Then you'd get stuck, and you don't want to damage the heart, so you have to hold firing and get to the next location. We talked through all that."

There was also the issue of video games' public image. At the time, games were seen more or less as the "enemy of civilization," as Cole remembered. Games had been blamed for the Columbine High School shootings in 1999.[1] Two years later, Rockstar's Grand Theft Auto III (GTA III) generated heated debate about the violence and sexual content in games, with many claiming that the game glorified, even encouraged, criminal behavior.[2] Violent games became the subject of frequent media reports. On June 25, 2003, teenagers William and Josh Buckner shot and killed Aaron Hamel and wounded Kimberly Bede; they later said they had been inspired by GTA III. That October, Hamel and Bede's families filed a $246 million lawsuit against Rockstar Games[3] and the companies associated with distributing the game. US senators began referencing studies on violent games and aggression. (There remains no definite link between the two. Some studies argue that video games have a negative impact on the behavior of young adults; however, in some cases, these conclusions were drawn from isolated incidents[4] involving randomly chosen participants who showed mild signs of aggression and antisocial behavior *immediately after* playing violent video games—behavior such as cutting off the people in front of them while walking out of the study or not saying "please" or "thank you." The conclusion drawn by the American Psychological Association, which recently reviewed several studies published between 2005 and 2013, is that there is insufficient evidence to say conclusively that violent video games actually increase the risk of violent or criminal behavior.)[5]

According to Cole, these studies were often correct about the potential of interactivity to influence behavior—but incorrect about how that potential is realized. "Most video games are not very impactful, either positively or negatively. You really have to work hard to make a video game impact on someone's behavior—it's not actually an easy thing to do, in our experience. So I think the generalization that games routinely do this stuff is wrong."

Omidyar used the debate about violent games to her advantage: if some people worried that games had the power to motivate bad behavior, the best thing she could do was use the same argument to show that games could motivate good behavior. In 2001, she set up her own nonprofit, HopeLab. She reached out to physicians, patients, and their families to get insight and data regarding the struggles faced by young cancer patients. Then, she turned to the question of development and distribution. Should the studio work with outside developers, or hire a team in-house to design the game?

After testing out several game concepts on young cancer patients at Lucile Packard Children's Hospital, HopeLab settled on a final design from a Los Angeles–based game design studio called Real Time Associates. The first version of Re-Mission was completed in 2005, but Omidyar wanted one more assurance that she was on the right track before releasing the game. Specifically, she wanted the support, and respect, of the medical community.

So, in mid-2005, she assembled a large randomized controlled trial of Re-Mission. Participants in randomized controlled trials are designated at random to receive one of three things: the clinical intervention (a drug, or, in this case, a video game) being tested; a placebo; and no intervention at all. "A randomized controlled trial was, and still is, the gold standard for testing," Cole said.

Cole began the "gargantuan struggle" of coordinating a team of 34 different medical centers across the United States, Canada, and Australia, each recruiting teenage cancer patients. The population of adolescent and young adults with cancer is relatively small, meaning that in order to get the sample size needed for a randomized clinical trial, HopeLab needed to recruit from a large sample size. The final number of patients—374—seems small, yet it made the study one of the first and largest to focus on adolescent cancer patients. HopeLab managed to secure funding for the trial from the National Cancer Institute, which told Omidyar she was crazy for trying to do the whole thing in a year. It would take at least five, they said.

During the study, patients were asked to play Re-Mission as much as they wanted to, with the stipulation that they play at least once a day. At Stanford, Dahl approached Lore to help him recruit patients. "It took a while for some of the younger patients to get it, but a lot of the older kids responded to it," Lore said. "The point was to teach them about their treatment—so, for example, yes, the chemo makes you feel bad, but at the same time, this is why we need to do it. This is why you lose your hair."

In the end, the study was completed in under a year, as Omidyar wanted. What's more, it proved that her assertions about the game were correct.[6] The control group received PCs preloaded with a popular video game; the rest of the participants received PCs with the same popular video game, plus a copy of Re-Mission. It was Kato's belief that the kids who played Re-Mission would be less hesitant about their cancer treatment and overall show more determination to get better. After three months, the research team found that the patients who had played Re-Mission had taken their antibiotics more consistently and with less resistance or complaint and that they had maintained higher levels of chemotherapy in their blood than those in the control group. The Re-Mission kids also seemed to know a lot more about their cancer, after the study was finished, than the control group—such as the names of particular cells and the biological processes involved in each of their treatments. (The results of the study were published in the peer-reviewed medical journal *Pediatrics*.)

But while the game seemed to be working, in the sense that patients who played it were paying more attention to their treatment and seemed to be more motivated to take their medications, it was hard to tell where the self-advocacy was coming from: the textual information in the game, or the act of playing the game? (The game was preloaded with all kinds of information, including some possibly overlong cutscenes about all the bad things that would happen to Roxxi if she didn't take her medicine, and so on.) Was it possible to separate the information from the motivation and see which was having a stronger effect?

Around this time, Cole officially joined HopeLab as the vice president of research and development. After studying the results of the study closely, Cole reasoned that the motivation, rather than the information, was having greater impact. To test this theory, HopeLab partnered with Stanford to conduct a functional magnetic resonance imaging (fMRI) study in which the brain activity of patients playing Re-Mission was monitored and compared with that of patients who were only watching the game. The results, published in the journal *PLoS One* in March 2012,[7] showed that neural circuits in the brain related to reward and motivation lit up in those who played Re-Mission but not in those who simply watched, explaining why active players were more likely to change their behavior and attitudes in relation to their treatment.

Cole paid close attention to see whether it was the information-processing region of the brain, or regions having to do with sustained positive motivation and goal-seeking, that lit up when patients played Re-Mission. "By the time we had done all of these follow-up studies, we were pretty convinced that it was really about that act of playing itself—the chasing cancer cells and learning more about them and getting further in the game—which was turbo-charging the good behavior in the patients."

It seemed unlikely that the patients were forgetting how to take their maintenance chemotherapy, or forgetting the basic principle that maintenance chemotherapy is important for fighting cancer. They all knew all this. More information would not be helpful. However, making kids feel like maintenance chemotherapy was a kind of ammunition for a gun or rocket launcher that they could use to fight this epic foe threatening their well-being was a different story. There was also the active-versus-passive element: why weren't the kids who were watching the game experiencing the same positive behavioral changes as those who were playing it? "The empirical answer is if you watch something passively, your visual cortex lights up—you know the information is coming in," said Cole. "What's different is where that information goes." In other words, how does the brain utilize that information? The area of the brain particularly responsive in participants playing Re-Mission was the area that drives goal-seeking behavior.

Once people know they are in charge of an outcome, they will fight hard to win, even if they don't particularly care about what they are winning. "I mean, you can give them a dead fish at the end of the day, they don't care—they just want to win the game." Game-playing participants also appeared more aroused—their brains were moving information around much more quickly, and to more places, than the brains of non-game-playing participants. Finally, Cole noticed that the hippocampi of game-playing participants were lighting up pretty regularly, compared with those of non-game-playing participants (the hippocampus being the center of emotion and memory in the brain), meaning that those playing the game were much more likely to form long-term memories of their experiences than those simply watching. "So if you wanted to take a piece of information, get it into a person, and then have them do something that is going to stick with them over time, these are the three things you'd really like most to see. One, a lot of positive motivation to do something with the information; two, evidence that their brain was moving the information around and processing it; and three, some proof that their brain was steering this information into long-term memory."

Jo Lennan, a close friend of ours was diagnosed with cancer two years ago. She is 32. She underwent eight months of chemotherapy starting in November 2014. After one surgery, her doctors gave her a choice: continue taking ketamine, a mild painkiller that can cause hallucinations and nightmares, or switch to a stronger drug. Lennan chose to stick with ketamine, even after experiencing a particularly bad nightmare. The experience was rare, she said. "It doesn't come naturally to some doctors to empower their patients' choices. More often, they would prefer to weigh things up themselves and then let you know what you'll be doing. As human beings, though, we usually want reasons to do things, and 'Because I say so' isn't as illuminating or motivating as knowledge can be. That's as true for kids as it is for adults."

Re-Mission was released in 2006 to nearly unanimous praise from the international medical community. The encouraging results of both studies led HopeLab to invest in Re-Mission 2, a collection of free online games playable both in browsers and on mobile platforms that adhere to the same principles as the original, only with more gameplay and fewer informational cutscenes. Game levels start out shorter and easier, game objectives are clearer, and targets more obvious. The gameplay is optimized to help players feel a sense of quick initial accomplishment and progressive growth in skills. The intention was to make Re-Mission 2 easier to play and thus have it appeal to a wide range of ages and genders.

By switching to a series of mini-games, HopeLab was also able to develop Re-Mission 2 at much less cost (Cole estimates that the cost of developing Re-Mission 2 was one-tenth that of Re-Mission) and use multiple game designers to ultimately create a variety of different gameplay styles. The switch also allowed Hope-Lab to perform user testing progressively throughout the game-development process, rather than waiting until the game was complete and hoping that it worked.

Both Re-Mission and Re-Mission 2 are currently available for free to young cancer patients and institutions in over 80 countries. At the time of writing, more than 210,000 copies of the original Re-Mission have been distributed; Re-Mission 2 game downloads have also surpassed the 200,000 mark and more than 400,000 game levels have been completed by players.[8]

"This whole venture of doing a serious game was really a shot in the dark," Kato said recently. "We knew we wanted to focus on adherence, and we knew you can't get that out of showing someone a video or telling them or writing a brochure. If you're a kid with cancer, it's scary. You know you're supposed to take your pills. You know if you do it you will live longer. But when you take your pill for chemo, the immediate reward is that your hair falls out, your face blows up, and you're sick all the time. Re-Mission made it empowering to have to go through all this. It made the kids feel like they were in control, for once."

HOPELAB'S SUCCESS WITH THE Re-Mission games inspired the studio to broaden its focus to other areas that might benefit from video game solutions. Looking at the landscape of health issues involving youth, HopeLab settled on childhood obesity, a growing problem increasingly cited by health experts as a danger to the health of Americans today. According to the US Centers for Disease Control and Prevention, childhood obesity has more than doubled in the last 30 years; in 2012, more than one-third of children and adolescents were overweight or obese.[9]

The Re-Mission studies had proven that it was possible for a video game to influence behavior in young people positively. Fred Dillon, HopeLab's director of product development, has helped steer the company away from sick care and toward prevention. "Rather than focusing on helping young adults fight a disease once it has already taken hold, we realized we could actually create tools that support health and well-being early in life, and help keep them healthy," Dillon told us.

To better understand the target demographic, HopeLab interviewed 25 middle-schoolers around the country about everything from their eating and exercise habits to their preferred leisure activities. "It's the age when kids start to figure out whether they're a sport kid or not," Dillon said. The studio then identified where a game would be likely to have greater impact: was it on the eating-and-calories part of things, or the exercise part?

Ultimately, the decision was that it would be much easier to motivate kids to exercise than to get them interested in nutrition, particularly as kids often have little control over what they eat in the first place. HopeLab also wanted to hear from the kids themselves, so the studio launched a competition asking children to submit ideas for products that would increase physical activity. A lot of what came back was based on a simple action-reward structure: one kid submitted an idea for a version of Dance Dance Revolution, but with texting—so kids would text with their feet.

The result was a platform of games named Zamzee, whose aim is to measure kids' physical activity and reward them for it. Kids (and their families) can earn gift cards through the platform for completing certain physical challenges. The rewards range from monetary (gift cards at a $5 value to sites like Amazon or iTunes) to pro-social (contributions to a selected charity—ASPCA, the participant's school, Save the Children, and so on) to virtual rewards (avatar items and graphical "badges" that appear on players' home screens).

Early pilot tests conducted in partnership with local schools and universities showed an increase in physical activity of up to 30 percent. Usually, pilot tests lasted from 6 to 12 weeks, with 60 to 100 kids. In a six-month, 448-person randomized controlled study, HopeLab found that kids playing Zamzee were 59 percent more active than those in the control group.[10] (That's the equivalent of doing an extra 45 minutes of nonstop pushups each week.)

It's Dillon's wish that HopeLab broadens its focus beyond gaming. This means working with everyone from for-profit organizations to health care providers to universities—anyone with a vision for using technology and games to improve areas like health and psychology. Recently, the lab partnered with the Yale Center for Emotional Intelligence to create an app that tracks users' moods throughout the day. Called the Mood Meter, it was originally based on a visual aid in Yale classrooms. The app enables users to plot their feelings and select strategies to manage each feeling. Users can also schedule reminders throughout the day to update the app on their mood changes. "We'll work with anybody who wants to make the world a better place," Cole, who is still with HopeLab, says.

BACK AT LUCILE PACKARD Hospital, Lore took us to visit Andrew, a 12-year-old whose leukemia had relapsed. Andrew eyed the iPad hungrily as Lore approached, conceding that while Re-Mission 2 is hard, he likes it because it gets his brain moving. "It does make you think about [cancer]. It gives you a better idea of what's going on inside your body." Later, Lore visited Mirella, a seven-year-old with leukemia, in the room next door to Andrew's. She was in the middle of an argument with her mother about taking her liquid Tylenol. She said it tasted bad. Mirella lay curled in the fetal position on the bed, her small, hairless head the only thing visible above the blankets. She eyed Lore apprehensively as he approached. "Look, Mirella, I've got a game for you." She saw the iPad in his hands and reacted instinctively, throwing the covers off and sitting upright.

Lore handed her the iPad and asked if she'd be interested in playing a new game that would help her feel better about her cancer. She nodded, and Lore clicked on the Re-Mission 2 icon. She began playing without waiting for Lore's instructions, getting the hang of the game as she went along. Every time Lore would explain something, she would just nod, her eyes glued to the screen.

Mirella's mother watched. "What did you say this game was called?" she asked Lore. Lore explained the concept. "We sometimes use it to help kids understand what cancer is and why it's important for them to keep fighting," he said, talking to Mirella's mother but keeping his eyes on his young patient.

After ten minutes, Lore told Mirella it was time to take the iPad to another patient. "Did you like the game?" he asked her. She nodded, not unenthusiastically. "Now," Lore continued, "how about that Tylenol? It won't taste so bad, right?"

Mirella threw him a look, as if to say, I know exactly what you're doing, and it won't work. But when her mother picked up the syringe of bright pink liquid, she didn't protest.

7.

Armchair Scientists

(THE STORY OF FOLDIT AND CROWDGAMING)

I n September 2011, the scientific journal *Nature Structural and Molecular Biology*[1] published the results of a rather strange experiment. It detailed how a group of ten gamers with no background in science had managed to solve a biochemical problem surrounding the AIDS-causing monkey virus known as Mason-Pfizer. The problem had eluded scientists and supercomputers for more than 15 years. The gamers had solved it in just ten days.

They had achieved their feat using an online puzzle game called Foldit, created in 2008 by a research team at the University of Washington in Seattle to test the hypothesis that crowdgaming could be used to solve different kinds of scientific problems. Anyone can sign up to play Foldit, which matches players into teams and presents each team with a different puzzle involving protein structures. The aim is to fold proteins in different ways until they fit together to "solve" a particular structure. Each structure relates to a particular biochemical problem—like the Mason-Pfizer virus, for example. Once a team of players submits a solved structure in Foldit, it is then analyzed by a team of University of Washington scientists to determine its validity.

Think of it like a virtual lab, where everyone works in round-the-clock shifts, taking over where the last group left off.

Foldit's players—and there are over a hundred thousand at last count—are everyday people interested in science.[2] Some are electricians. Others are lawyers. There are even a few grandmothers. Recently, the University of Washington team behind Foldit created a new game, called NanoCrafter, with a similar concept. Instead of folding proteins, NanoCrafter players are asked to reconfigure molecular structures. The team is working on porting both games to smartphones and tablets, to give players more freedom to choose when and where they play.

The hope is that one day, citizen scientists from around the world will be making discoveries as impactful as the Mason-Pfizer solution on a daily basis.

CITIZEN SCIENCE IS NOT exactly a new concept. Scientists have been enlisting the help of large groups of people since the nineteenth century, mostly for the purposes of data collection: everything from tracking weather systems to monitoring bird populations and hunting for fossils. In fact, at one point, that was the conventional way of doing scientific work. But as data collection and analysis became increasingly digitized in the twentieth century, research slowly retreated back to the lab. Then, around 1996, a few adventurous souls in the field of psychology decided to try web-based testing: quick online surveys that could be completed anytime, anywhere, eliminating the costly and time-consuming ritual of finding participants and bringing them into a physical location. As internet access spread, the kinds of people signing up for the surveys diversified. At first, it was mostly science buffs or those with a vested interest in the research; then, more and more people began participating, for reasons scientists could only guess at. They were bored? Curious? They wanted to help science in some way? With no way of knowing, some scientists, particularly the old guard, became increasingly skeptical at the notion of collecting data in this seemingly haphazard way. Who knew who these people responding to these surveys were? They could be hackers. They could be answering the questions with the intent of influencing the results. They could be science skeptics, intent on sabotaging the scientific method.

At its core, the scientific method is about control. Specifically, it's about controlling variables and making sure each and every piece of the puzzle is accounted for. Then, one can manipulate one tiny piece to see what it does and how it can affect the overall picture. The method is crucial to testing scientific theories, so studies are usually designed within a tightly controlled context—a soundproof room with a closed door, or a single computer with a single program. Only then do scientists step out into the real world to see if the results can be replicated.

But it's often hard to apply the results obtained in this kind of environment to the real world, where things are messy and chaotic. This is why some scientists thought the internet might be a good middle ground. Then, two important things changed. First, the internet ceased (for the most part, anyway) to be a dark, scary pit in which the worst of humanity went to hide; and second, those very same skeptics suddenly could not live without it. Online culture blossomed. Smartphones became ubiquitous. Netflix sprang up. "The people who didn't really understand the social culture of the internet are now part of it," says Laura Germine, a postdoctoral fellow in the Psychiatric and Neurodevelopmental Genetics Unit at Massachusetts General Hospital and Harvard Medical School. Her work revolves around observing how social abilities are distinct from other cognitive abilities and why some people are more vulnerable than others to developing mental disorders.

While still a grad student, Germine began working in a lab where researchers were studying a condition known colloquially as "face blindness." The disorder, now relatively well known thanks to the work of neurologists, including the late Oliver Sacks, who wrote extensively on the subject in his best-selling book *The Man Who Mistook His Wife for a Hat*, was at the time still somewhat obscure.[3] In the 1990s, a small group of people began to gather in online medical forums to complain about the difficulty they had in recognizing faces, including those of friends and even spouses. The medical community was skeptical. These people had not suffered any major brain trauma or damage that could possibly cause such a strange neurological glitch. The group continued to search for someone who would take them seriously, eventually stumbling upon a man named Brad Duchaine, a postdoctoral fellow at the Vision Sciences Laboratory at Harvard who later moved overseas to lecture in psychology at the University College London. Duchaine was already investigating face blindness, trying to figure out how real it was and what caused it. By the time Germine joined his lab in 2005, Duchaine was being contacted by hundreds of people around the world asking to get involved. Germine and Duchaine began flying people to London for testing and sending them home with written confirmation of just how bad they were at recognizing faces. "That was really important for a lot of these people, because some of them had gone their whole lives just thinking they were really stupid or incompetent, when really they had a very specific problem," Germine says.

When the number of people writing in became overwhelming, Germine and Duchaine developed a simpler version of the test to put online, so that anyone could take it at home. At the time, they didn't think of the test as a data collection tool; it was more like a community outreach service. They emailed the link to the few hundred people who had written in. A few weeks later, their website crashed; instead of a few hundred people, close to 15,000 had tried to log in. Germine and Duchaine had an idea: What if you made a cognitive lab test "playable" and put it online? Who would respond?

The pair mined the data collected from the online face-blindness test and found a completely normal distribution of scores—low, high, and everything in between. The result obeyed the statistical rules of a random data sample—exactly as one would expect if all 15,000 people had come into the lab individually. "So we said okay," Germine says. "Maybe this is a way that we could do science."

Later, in 2008, Germine founded Testmybrain.org, an online portal for testing and research data collection. She adapted the cognitive tests from the lab, making them simple, fun, and interesting and building feedback tools so people could immediately see their scores and tell researchers what they liked and didn't like about the tests. Testmybrain.org includes normal puzzle tests, fill-in-the-blanks tests, picture-recognition tests, spot-the-difference tests, and so on. Since the site launched, 1.5 million people from around the world have taken tests on Testmybrain.org. Germine says there are roughly 50 domains being developed currently; there are tests for almost everything, from cognition and intellectual function to diabetes, neurological disorders, and even simple aging. Any research team or university interested in utilizing web-based testing can sign up.

More than 20 papers have been published based on data sets fromTestmybrain.org tests. Topics include how the brain changes over the lifespan; the correlation between childhood experiences and social abilities; how face recognition peaks in the early thirties; and how fast people can visually estimate quantities depending on their ages. One study looked at our preferences for human attractiveness: do we all find the same faces attractive regardless of circumstance, or are our preferences shaped by our childhood and environment? It appears that the latter is the case: while most people agreed that Brad Pitt is better looking than Donald Trump, there were differences of opinion when it came to choosing between Pitt and George Clooney.[4] One study, named in *Forbes*' Top Ten Brain Science and Psychology Studies of 2015, showed that not all mental abilities peak and decline at a certain age—that some peak while we're young, while others peak when we are old. The study, published in *Psychological Science*, was significant due to the sheer number of participants involved: 50,000 people, from teens to those over 70. (Compare this with a traditional lab study, in which a sample size of more than 500 people is considered to be impressive.) The study showed that mental abilities such as brain processing do indeed peak around age 18, but some abilities, among them vocabulary skills, continue developing into old age, peaking around age 65.[5] Germine told *Forbes*:[6] "[The study] paints a different picture of the way we change over the lifespan than psychology and neuroscience have traditionally painted." The demand from the scientific community for Germine's web tests has grown so overwhelming that she recently formed a nonprofit, also called Test My Brain, to better facilitate the interaction between researchers and the public.

So who are the people who sign up to do these tests? Are they interested in science? Gaming? Do they genuinely want to help humanity, or are they just bored? According to Germine, who has spent a lot of time combing through Testmybrain.org user feedback, while many people do genuinely enjoy the idea that they are in a small way contributing to the greater good, the most common motivation is to learn a little something about themselves. Consider, for example, the number of people who take BuzzFeed quizzes like *Which Disney Princess Are You?* or *What's Your Spirit Color?* Most people know that the insights provided by these quizzes are shallow at best. But still, we take them. Why? Because the answers, no matter how trivial, give us some small knowledge of ourselves. "People feel intrinsically rewarded by [that]," Germine said. "It's also fun. We've all heard that joke about mankind creating this brilliant thing called the internet, which we now use to share cat pictures. The joke—and the truth it contains—simply speaks to our innate desire to play and share. So why not leverage it? "You can use these motivations to drive traffic to your study and make your study better—make it fun, accessible, interesting, and shareable," Germine says. "Then you've created a whole new set of motivations, which means your study is going to reach a much broader range of people. If we ignore those people, we're ignoring a huge portion of society—most of it, really."

The reverberations are being felt in the wider scientific community. There's been a slow shift in the acceptance of citizen science, aided in part by federal organizations including the National Institute of Health and the White House, which has been pushing the idea that science should be more inclusive and accessible. "What that accessibility means now is that researchers are finally beginning to understand the importance of deployed common technology in research studies," Germine says. "But this has only become an accepted way to do science in the last three years or so."

ONE OF THE MOST successful examples of citizen science is Lab in the Wild, an experimental platform for conducting online behavioral experiments. It was launched in 2012 by Krzysztof Gajos, an associate professor of computer science at Harvard University's School of Engineering and Applied Sciences, with the help of one of his postdoctoral researchers, Katharina Reinecke. The platform administers game-like tests online to unpaid volunteers. At the time of launch, Gajos was interested in observing how humans interact with computational systems, particularly how online interfaces can better accommodate people's varying abilities to see, hear, and interact.

Lab in the Wild launched with three studies, the most successful of which asked participants to rate a number of websites, on a scale of 1 to 9, based on visual appeal; more than 40,000 people from some 200 countries participated in the study, varying in age from 6 to 99. "We had everyone from scientists to plumbers take part," Reinecke said. The results of the study supported Reinecke's theory that what users perceive as "good" design is subject to individual and cultural preferences.[7] For example, the level of colorfulness and visual complexity people prefer varies wildly: according to the study, women like colorful websites more than men, while a highly educated person generally prefers less color. Russians prefer lower visual complexity, while Macedonians like highly intricate designs. Later, Gajos and Reinecke published a paper on Lab in the Wild,[8] in which they compared three experiments performed on the platform with similar studies done inside the lab, concluding that the online results replicated the in-lab studies with "comparable data quality." They concluded: "In comparison to conventional in-lab studies, Lab in the Wild enables the recruitment of participants at larger scale and from more diverse demographic and geographic backgrounds."

Some people would argue that games like Foldit and the activities found on Testmybrain.org and Lab in the Wild aren't really games. Not in the traditional sense, anyway. Few people would choose to play Foldit over Tetris based on technical elements and entertainment value, for example. But that doesn't necessarily exclude Foldit and the others from the category of games. The boundaries of game design have been slowly shifting and stretching over the last five years to include more experimental and innovative projects. Could a game like Foldit be better designed? Undoubtedly. But the fact that the game needs to deliver on a very specific objective—in this instance, a scientific one—limits what the game can be in the end, and it's therefore hard to say how much better, from a pure gaming standpoint, it could be.

However, if these games could be designed to be *more* entertaining, that would certainly increase their impact, because even more people would want to play them. "I don't *want* my documentary to be boring. It may have to be boring in parts to make a point, but that's never the goal," said Nicholas Fortugno, lead designer of the wildly popular game Diner Dash and the cofounder of the New York City–based game development studio Playmatics. "Better design makes better games, and the better the game is, the more it's played. If the game has social impact, then of course you want it played as much as possible. The fact that a lot of people played it is a triumph that shouldn't be overlooked, but it didn't live up to its potential if better design would let [even] more people access it."

Fortugno believes that many of these games would benefit from the touch of a professional game designer. This isn't to say that good games never come from amateurs—rather, that game expertise can make a game more appealing. Whether the games should be commercial is a different question. "I think that the question of money has little to no bearing on how fun the experience is. A good, serious game should make the high-end goal itself fun to achieve through [its] mechanics."

Reinecke didn't go out of her way to attract people to Lab in the Wild; instead, participants had the option of sharing the results of their tests online, which many did, inspiring others to take the test. Today, the site averages around 1,000 participants per day. There are usually only six to nine studies live on the site at any one time; researchers can submit their studies for preapproval, after which Lab in the Wild posts the studies to its Facebook page and asks users for their feedback. If the response is positive, the study goes up. The only rule is that studies have to be fun, simple, and shareable. One of the site's most popular studies was a test that guessed users' ages based on their clicking speeds; it attracted more than a million participants in its first two months.[9] The site also provides users with personalized feedback, allowing each participant to compare him or herself with users in other countries. This is probably why Lab in the Wild has had so much success on social media—currently, the majority of the site's traffic comes from Facebook. (The top user countries are usually the United States, the United Kingdom, Canada, Romania, and Hungary.) "I know of other successful citizen science and crowdsourcing projects where the people involved are really in it to help the world," Reinecke says. "With us, it's the opposite. It's less about altruism, and more about personal motivation—but hey, whatever works, right?"

CHRIS LINTOTT, AN ASTROPHYSICS professor at Oxford University, has been trying since 2007 to figure out what motivates citizen scientists. On a balmy summer evening in late July 2007, Lintott knocked off work early and went downstairs to the Royal

Oak, the pub across the road from the campus's Radcliffe Observatory, with his former student, Kevin Schawinski. As they talked about their week, Schawinski began to complain about his workload. He was in the middle of testing a theory that stars could be formed just as readily in older galaxies as in new ones. Unfortunately for Schawinski, the only way to test this theory was to sort manually through satellite photos to identify the varying characteristics of one million different galaxies. The age of a galaxy can be determined by its shape: elliptical usually means old, while spiral signifies a younger, more nubile galaxy. But since computers could not yet be trusted to identify these patterns correctly, Schawinski had sat at his desk for the last 30 days, 12 hours a day, looking at photographs. He was up to 50,000. At this rate, he could finish in less than two years. But what if he made a mistake? What if, late at night in his office, bleary-eyed and sleep-deprived, he misidentified a pattern? To ensure against misidentification, at least 20 other people had to go over each of the features Schawinski identified before a galaxy could safely be categorized—which meant that it would take more like three to five years to categorize all one million photographs.

Seeing the desperation in Schawinski's eyes, Lintott made a suggestion. Did Schawinski remember NASA's Stardust at Home project from 2006? In which the organization had posted satellite pictures and asked people to help identify interstellar dust? Yes, Schawinski said. He did. So why not try the same thing with the galaxies?

A couple of weeks later, Lintott and Schawinski launched Galaxy Zoo. They put up one million pictures of galaxies and some very simple instructions. Pick a picture, study the image of the colorful swirls within it, and then answer a series of questions, such as: Is the galaxy pictured elliptical or spiral? Smooth or tumescent? If a galaxy is spiral, are its spirals packed closely together, or are they loose and relaxed? Within 24 hours, the site was receiving 70,000 classifications per hour. The initial set of one million galaxies was classified in three weeks; in the first year of the project, more than 50 million classifications were received, from more than 150,000 people. And the accuracy problem? Solved. The sheer number of respondents per hour, looking at the same images, meant that Lintott and Schawinski could be certain no errors were made. "We had succeeded in creating the world's most powerful pattern-recognizing super-computer, and it existed in the linked intelligence of all the people who had logged on to our website: and this global brain was processing this stuff incredibly fast and incredibly accurately," Schawinski later told the *Guardian*.[10]

Galaxy Zoo soon expanded; Lintott's team developed a German and Polish-language version, and in 2009, Galaxy Zoo 2 was launched, with the task of identifying another quarter of a million galaxies. The first major discovery came in April 2009, when Schawinski, who had left Oxford the previous year to take up a new post as a postdoctoral research associate at Yale, discovered a forum thread on Galaxy Zoo in which a number of users—"Zooites," as they call themselves—were talking about a set of galaxies notable for their small size and bright green color. Schawinski asked a volunteer to take a closer look, and it was soon discovered that the "pea galaxies" were forming stars at ten times the rate of the Milky Way, and were therefore possibly the last remnants of a mode of star formation common in the early universe. A paper based on the volunteers' work on the so-called Peas was published later that year in the peer-reviewed journal *The Monthly Notices of the Royal Astronomical Society*.[11] (Since 2009, further study of the galaxies has proved the Peas to be invaluable as a "living fossil of galaxy evolution." "Because they aren't too far away, they provide a unique local laboratory in which we can investigate processes key to the formation and evolution of galaxies in the early universe," a Zooite wrote on the Galaxy Zoo blog. "They are undergoing extraordinary, intense starbursts unlike any other galaxies known in the local universe.")

To date, 48 papers based on Galaxy Zoo classifications and discoveries have been published in peer-reviewed journals. In 2015 alone, the site collected some 4.75 million classifications on more than 200,000 different images of galaxies.[12] On July 12, 2015, Lintott wrote a post on the Galaxy Zoo site to commemorate its eighth birthday. "I'm writing this on my way to report on the arrival of *New Horizons* at Pluto for the *Sky at Night*," he wrote,[13] referencing the long-running BBC series he now hosts. "For the first time, we'll see close-up images of a world that until now has been little more than a point of light. We need not travel to distant galaxies to understand them; encountering something new and never-before-seen in your web browser is thrill enough."

After the early success of Galaxy Zoo, Lintott realized the potential for using his Zooites to do other kinds of science. Plus, researchers from all over the world were contacting him to ask if they could borrow the Zooites to look through *their* data. In 2009, Lintott proposed a new platform called Zooniverse, which would allow citizen scientists to work on all kinds of projects and tasks, not just those that were astronomy-related, and convened a sort of war council made up of representatives from seven institutions in the United Kingdom and the United States, including Oxford University, Johns Hopkins University, the Adler Planetarium, and the National Maritime Museum.

Calling themselves the Citizen Science Alliance, the group launched Zooniverse the same year, pulling together projects from different scientific fields, including astronomy, ecology, cell biology, and climate science. There's Cell Slider, in which volunteers help classify archived cancer cell samples from images provided by Cancer Research UK; a project aimed at annotating images such as photographs of wild orchids from the Natural History Museum in London; sound-based projects, among which is one devoted to monitoring the status of bat populations by classifying audio files recorded in the wild; and perennially fascinating projects like those for counting craters on Mars or extracting weather records from the logbooks of Arctic expedition ships to better catalogue the onset of climate change. With 1.5 million registered volunteers, Zooniverse is now one of the largest citizen science projects online. Some 100 papers have been published based on Zooniverse discoveries alone.[14]

And again, although Zooniverse projects are not defined as games in the traditional sense, there are many overlaps with game design and mechanics. One is the tension between scientific efficiency and a good user experience. The projects that do best are often those with a clear objective, something like: "If you sort through x, we will discover y." Sometimes, volunteers' reaction to a project leaves Lintott scratching his head. Take a project called Snapshot Serengeti, for example, for which users have to classify animals in Serengeti National Park in Tanzania based on images gathered from motion-sensitive cameras across the park. When the project first kicked off, Lintott and his team noticed that about two-thirds of the images didn't have any animals in them—either the cameras had malfunctioned or something else had set them off. So they collected all the blank images and removed them from the project, thinking they were improving users' experience by removing dud images. But as soon as they did, interest in the project dropped dramatically. It seemed that *nothing-nothing-nothing-zebra!* was much more exciting than *zebra-zebra-zebra-wildebeest!* What Lintott had witnessed was the psychology of variable rewards in action, much as it was in B. F. Skinner's famous experiment in the 1950s, in which he trained lab mice to press levers for treats. In one experiment, he gave one group of mice a treat every time they pressed the lever, while another group was consistently kept on its toes, sometimes getting treats, other times getting nothing. Surprisingly, it was the second group that compulsively pressed the lever—the uncertainty of the result being more exciting than always knowing exactly what was coming. Lintott: "That complexity of interaction consistently surprises me."

As do the continual discoveries of hardworking Zooites. The latest to cause a stir occurred in 2015, with a project called Planet Hunters. The project's purpose is to find planets around other stars by looking at images snapped by NASA's Kepler telescope. Users are on the lookout for a "blink"—the momentary dimming of a star, which indicates that a planet may have passed in front of it.

If there's a pattern of repeated blinks, one can get increasingly confident that there is indeed a planet there. In October 2015, volunteers identified what has since been labeled the most interesting star in the galaxy, sending the astronomical world into a tizzy. It happened like this: a star, KIC 8462852, blinked randomly a couple of times and then did nothing for a year. Next, it lost 20 percent of its light for an hour and then did nothing for another year. Then it went on a blinking rampage. No one had any idea what was going on. Naturally, the early theory—which attracted sizable media attention, from publications ranging from the *Daily Mail*[15] to the *New Yorker*[16]—involved aliens. (SETI, the search for extraterrestrial intelligence, got involved at one point, listening for any alien transmissions, and found none.) Later, it was pointed out that a computer alone could not have made the discovery; citizen science was praised once more.[17] (As for the blinking star, the mystery remains unsolved. Lintott concedes: "I don't think it's aliens, but it's something very unusual.")

In 2015, Lintott and his team introduced a new version of the Zooniverse software, which included a project-building tool. The aim was to allow any Zooite to build his or her own project, share it with the wider community, and submit it for review to be launched sitewide. A volunteer beta team was assembled to check all new incoming projects and flag any usability issues. According to Lintott, the idea was to involve the crowd at a much earlier stage. "We're now collaborating with the volunteers, instead of simply assigning them stuff. They are in control of what science is done."

This suggests that Lintott has a great deal of trust in his Zooites. But volunteers are, after all, volunteers. They are not scientists. So how can they be trusted to come up with scientifically sound projects? When Galaxy Zoo launched, Lintott assumed most people were flocking to the site because they thought the pictures were pretty. As it turns out, the images weren't the exciting part: it was more the idea that the volunteers could make a valuable contribution to science. (This makes an interesting contrast to what Germine and Reinecke found, which was that users reported being motivated by self-discovery or competition.)

When Lintott and Schawinski conducted a survey of 11,000 Zooites in 2008 to find out more about their ages, locations, and motivations for signing up, nearly half said their primary goal was to be involved in useful research. (The survey also showed that 80 percent of Zooites are men.) For the other half, the attraction was the sheer wonder of it all. Most Zooites are not hard-core science nerds; Lintott said they're more like the kind of people who pause when they see an article in the newspaper about a new galaxy—but not the kind who would ever go to an amateur astronomy meeting or seek out the science museum when visiting a new city. "Every galaxy has a story to tell," Aida Berges, a homemaker from Puerto Rico, told *Time* in 2010.[18] She had, at that point, classified 150,000 galaxies.

The point is that people don't necessarily have to be heavily interested in science to want to contribute to Zooniverse. (The exceptions are volunteers for the penguin-counting project, who were, Lintott says, exclusively interested in penguins.) Perhaps because of this, some Zooites often find themselves so fascinated by a particular project that they are inspired to do more. "When they find something interesting, they'll go on the web and get their own data, and do their own analysis and investigate what they find," Lintott says. "The projects almost act as a gateway for those who want to be more advanced." This is why Lintott trusts his Zooites so much. It's also the reason he wants to develop Zooniverse to the point where the platform can take advantage of these higher achievers. Right now, tasks are assigned randomly—one person is as likely to get an image of a particular galaxy as anyone else. But people have different skill sets and, as we've seen, varying levels of interest.

In order to cope with large data sets, Lintott believes, the platform will have to evolve to the point where it can isolate particular individuals in the crowd who are more suited than others to a particular task. In other words, personalizing the crowdsourcing experience. "So, you might be out shopping and get a message on your phone saying, 'We need you to classify four images, which we know only you, out of everyone online or available, can give the answer to.'"

The only thing that might stand in the way is machine learning. In the eight years since Galaxy Zoo launched, those with knowledge of the field have continually predicted that in just a few years' time, machines will be able to do what Zooites do. But this hasn't happened yet. The sense is that citizen science is useful now, but everyone is anticipating the day when machine learning will finally take over. "People are often betting we're going to go out of business," Lintott says. "So far, they've been wrong. And I think they'll continue to be wrong."

Occasionally, someone will point out that citizen science

involves a lot of citizen but not much science, since all people are doing is clicking on stuff on their computers. Lintott is always amused. "Anyone who has been a working scientist will tell you that science already involves a lot of that."

8.

Under the Hood

(THE STORY OF NEURORACER AND PROJECT EVO)

I n February 2013, a pale-skinned, shaggy-haired graduate of the DigiPen Institute of Technology launched a Kickstarter campaign[1] that sounded too good to be true: for $40,000, he would create a video game that would allow players to control objects with their minds. "Throw Trucks with Your Mind is a multiplayer-focused game where you . . . wait for it . . . throw trucks with your mind." The device that would allow players to do this was an EEG headset: an electrophysiological monitoring headset made up of tiny electrode sensors that, when placed along the scalp, can record electrical activity in the brain. (To get really technical: the device measures voltage fluctuations in the current that passes through neurons.)

It was Lat Ware's intention to create a video game in which players could control in-game virtual objects, like trucks, by focusing their mental energy on them. The more a player focused on a particular object, the harder he or she could throw it.

A first-person shooter game in a multiplayer setting, Throw Trucks with Your Mind is set in a colorful, cartoonish world wherein two opponents face off against each other. Since brain controls are such a foreign mechanism for most players, Ware wanted to keep the game itself firmly grounded in the familiar. The objective is to crush the other player's avatar—literally—by pulling, levitating, and throwing objects of various sizes and weights, using a combination of brainpower and traditional game controls. Players move with the W, A, S, and D keys, aim with the mouse, jump with the spacebar, switch between powers with numbers from 1 to 8, and activate a power by holding down the mouse button.

How far a player can throw an object is entirely dependent on his or her ability to stay calm and focus. "We designed the game to be as accessible to young children as possible, while still having a difficulty curve that's easy to learn but hard to master," Ware said. "We also replaced all instances of the words 'kill' and 'death' with 'squish.' When you squish someone, they disappear in a puff of smoke and reappear ten seconds later. Anyone who has played Minecraft will already be familiar with the controls."

Unlike traditional first-person shooter games, Throw Trucks with Your Mind isn't about speed; in fact, the more time players take to focus, the better they are likely to perform. Ware, 30, came up with the idea for a "first-person thinker" video game while at DigiPen, in Redmond, Washington, where he majored in computer science. After graduating, in 2007, he spent the next several years unsuccessfully trying to sell venture capitalists on the idea.

Finally, someone suggested he raise the money for the game through Kickstarter. He made a primitive prototype using a headset developed by a San Jose company called NeuroSky, then launched the campaign in February 2013. (NeuroSky is better known for partnering with toy manufacturer Uncle Milton in 2009 for the *Star Wars*–themed "Force Trainer" toy, in which players use an EEG-like headset to move a ball higher and higher into the air just by concentrating on it.)

Ware took his prototype to gaming conventions and developer meet-ups to drum up early support for his Kickstarter campaign. The gaming press took notice,[2] and six weeks after it launched, the Kickstarter campaign closed with a total of 584 backers and $47,287, beating Ware's original goal.

Ware grew up liking video games a lot more than he liked people. As a teenager, he underwent treatment for attention deficit disorder, or ADD. The treatment was neurofeedback therapy, which involves placing electrodes on a patient's scalp and displaying his or her brainwave activity on a screen. The idea is that, through practice, the patient can learn to control his or her brainwaves and change them to match the "normal" brainwaves of a non–ADD sufferer. "I had been on medication since kindergarten, and this was a wonderful alternative," Ware said.

It was also expensive, so Ware eventually had to stop. But not before he realized he could use neurofeedback to fulfill a childhood dream: to make the ultimate *Star Wars*–themed game, in which a player could control objects using his or her mind, just like a Jedi. When Ware was 19, he saw a NeuroSky demonstration of an EEG headset hooked up to a Half-Life 2 engine, which enabled the player to push things around and lift objects in the game. Unfortunately, the hardware cost $5,000. Eight years later, when NeuroSky released a version of the EEG headset that cost only $100, Ware bought two and got to work. He did a lot of what he calls "coffee shop development," asking random people to play various prototypes of the game, before he realized he could go no further without an art team. So, on October 1, 2012, he quit his job and began looking for a way to fund Throw Trucks with Your Mind.

Ware raised $12,000 in the first two days of the Kickstarter campaign, and then donations flatlined. "I realized five days in that the only people backing the game were the ones who'd already played it, so, in addition to hitting up every press site I could, I was going to two to four meetings a day, demoing for 30 to 50 people at each event. I am an introvert, so when I finally hit the goal, I collapsed into a ball on the living room floor and didn't move for the rest of the day."

Eventually, Ware hired five more developers and started a company, Crooked Tree Studios. He paid his team just enough to survive on and paid himself nothing. He couldn't afford rent, so he moved out of his apartment and couch-surfed for eight months while the game was in development. "I was completely up-front with everyone about the money situation," he said. After the Kickstarter campaign, he raised an additional $240,000 for development from angel investors and borrowed another $55,000 from family. For the most part, he said, people don't believe Throw Trucks with Your Mind is real until they play it. "I see about ten times more unfriendly skepticism than support. But among people who play it, almost everyone loves it."

Aside from the Jedi thing, Ware's motivation was to create a game that could help children who suffer from an attention disorder. "I did a lot of research on neurofeedback therapy and ended up building the game so that the techniques you master through ordinary gameplay are the same ones you use for treating attention deficit disorder, post-traumatic stress disorder, and anxiety." Ware is currently trying to prove that this works in a clinical setting, because, as he is well aware, it would be wrong to claim that the game can help until he can prove it actually does. "I dream of a world where children who are diagnosed with disorders are prescribed video games and that those games are covered by insurance."

WARE'S DREAM IS SHARED by Dr. Adam Gazzaley, a neurology professor at the University of California in San Francisco and director of the Gazzaley Lab. The lab is best known for using technology, especially video games, to thwart cognitive decline. For years, Gazzaley's work has focused on memory and attention—in particular, how these processes change with aging and dementia and what we can do to keep aging minds active. His lab couples behavioral assessments with techniques like functional magnetic resonance imaging (fMRI), electroencephalography (EEG), and transcranial magnetic stimulation (TMS).

In person, Gazzaley cuts a striking figure. He's tall and broad-shouldered, with a healthy crop of silver hair, dark brown eyes, and a placid demeanor. One might call him intimidating, but there's a keen sense of humor lurking beneath the surface, for those willing to tease it out. "Adam works really hard and plays really hard," Brett Morrison, a neurology resident at Johns Hopkins Hospital and a friend of Gazzaley's, once observed.[3]

Born in Brooklyn, Gazzaley developed an early interest in science as a devotee of Carl Sagan's *Cosmos* series on PBS. After competing in a statewide science fair with a project on solar energy, Gazzaley petitioned his parents to let him attend the Bronx High School of Science, despite the commute being nearly four hours round-trip by public transportation from his house in Howard Beach. He passed the admission test and spent the next four years getting up at 5:30 a.m. to catch a bus.

Gazzaley felt like very much the outsider—Howard Beach was a working-class neighborhood, and none of his friends understood his determination to go to college. After various Ivy League schools turned him down, Gazzaley was accepted into the State University of New York (SUNY) at Binghamton—where, in his sophomore year as a biochemistry major, he was nearly expelled for blowing up a toilet. (His plan to create a chemical reaction in the lake behind campus with a large piece of sodium metal backfired—literally—when he tested it first in a toilet block with 30 other students looking on. "All that was left was two pipes sticking out of the wall," he recalled. No one was hurt, but Gazzaley was placed on social probation—in other words, no parties.)

While trying to fulfill his humanities requirements, Gazzaley took a series of classes focused on different visions of the future; in one class, the lecturer showed students research on nanobots and how they might one day be used in neurosurgery to complement—if not entirely replace—a brain surgeon's hands. "It was almost like science fiction, and it just sparked this little bug in me," Gazzaley later recalled. He took out every textbook he could find on neuroscience, and later applied successfully to Mount Sinai School of Medicine's (MSSM) MD-PhD program.

Under the guidance of neurobiologist John Morrison, Gazzaley began looking into how aging alters cognitive function. While studying memory in a group of monkeys, Gazzaley developed a method for measuring changes in proteins called NMDA receptors, which play a role in memory formation. He published three papers between 1996 and 1997, which established that memory-related neural circuitry is not damaged by the process of aging, as it is in Alzheimer's disease. Instead, Gazzaley reasoned, the cause of memory loss due to simple aging seems to come from subtle molecular changes in the brain, which prevent neurons from communicating with one another the way they're supposed to.

That discovery was a significant achievement for a young scientist. According to Morrison, Gazzaley was able to master what few scientists his age could: not just successfully answering a research query with tested data, but producing publishable results. Another MSSM neuroscientist, Deanna Benson, said once that working with Gazzaley back then was more like working with a peer than with a student, despite her initial skepticism about his fashion sense: "He dressed in tank tops and shorts. He used to lift weights a lot, too, so he looked kind of all buffed out—like the kind of guy who spent more time in the gym than he ever would spend in the lab."

From 1999 to 2002, Gazzaley completed his residency in neurology at the University of Pennsylvania, where he met neurobiologist Mark D'Esposito, who at the time was using fMRI to study cognition. Gazzaley liked the idea of being able to visualize brain activity, and when D'Esposito later invited Gazzaley to come to California to do his postdoctoral training at UC Berkley, he accepted.

SOON AFTERWARD, GAZZALEY BECAME restless. His work to date had focused on things like distraction, multitasking, focus, decision making, and memory. What he had learned was that, while most people experience ups and downs within each of these areas, things get steadily worse as one ages. But, while the work was satisfying, something was missing. Namely, he hadn't found a way to fix the problem. "I felt that we weren't doing anything to help the people that are troubled by it and frustrated by it and maybe even impaired by it," he told us recently. "It was intellectually fascinating, but my goal has always been to help people."

This restlessness was also driven in part by Gazzaley's growing profile. He was giving as many as 70 talks a year and becoming increasingly embarrassed that none ended with any sense of hope. "I'd finish a talk and the [audience] would be like, 'Wait, that's it?' It was like a movie where everyone dies in the end and the credits roll. And it's, like, the worst movie of all time. No matter how good the story is, or how interesting it is, when you're in the audience, listening to this stuff, it's just not satisfying in any way to end with bad news."

There was already a growing movement around "brain training" games, which included games and apps like Dr. Kawashima's How Old Is Your Brain?, a popular puzzle game for the Nintendo

DS that single-handedly raised the median age of the console's user base by at least 20 years. But scientists were skeptical. In 2014, a group of leading cognitive psychologists and neuroscientists released a statement[4] warning that the scientific literature did not support the claims made by many brain-training apps and games, namely that they help prevent cognitive decline.

In early 2016, the company behind one of the most popular brain-training apps, Luminosity, agreed to pay $2 million to settle false marketing claims[5] that the app alleviated symptoms of Alzheimer's. The US Federal Trade Commission asked the company to contact its more than 70 million users and offer them the chance to cancel their subscriptions to some 40 online games. Despite this, the market shows no signs of slowing down: according to recent projections,[6] the global cognitive assessment and training market is expected to grow from $2.4 billion in 2015 to $7.5 billion by 2020 for digital and paper-based products combined. By comparison, the digital apps market is forecasted to reach $6 billion by 2020, according to a recent report[7] that also predicts that biometrics-aided meditation will be the next big thing in consumer wellness, with more than one million adults in North America expected to take self-administered annual brain health checkups via an iPad or Android tablet.

Gazzaley was one the scientists who signed the 2014 statement, but he later admitted[8] to having doubts, chiefly because he feared that such a bold move could scare off potential investors interested in funding further research into brain training projects. He wasn't interested in making a brain-training game per se, but he liked the idea of interactivity. He thought the solution needed to be more immersive—something that could deliver long-term benefits, not just immediate satisfaction.

One method would be to simply devise a series of cognitive tasks that players could perform over and over again. But this wouldn't take advantage of the brain's plasticity. When we are young, our brains are more plastic—we can learn multiple languages with speed and efficiency, for example. As we age, our brains become increasingly rigid—but it's still possible to get better at brain-related activities over time. "The big question was what type of interactivity is even tolerable to do for any amount of time," Gazzaley says. The second, equally important, question was, how do you repeatedly engage someone in an activity enough times to determine a long-term benefit, not just an immediate one?

To get answers, Gazzaley called Daphne Bavelier, a cognitive neuroscientist at the University of Geneva studying the real-world effects of video games. Born in Paris, Bavelier got her PhD at MIT, followed by a postdoctoral fellowship at the Salk Institute in San Diego, where she became interested in brain plasticity and learning. While conducting a study into the effects of age on peripheral vision, Bavelier found that all the subjects participating in the study, most of them students, achieved a nearly perfect score on certain digital field-of-view assessments.[9] "When we looked for commonalities between the pilot subjects, we found that all of them belonged to an action video game club," Bavelier said later. Working together with an undergraduate lab technician named Shawn Green, Bavelier switched the project to study the impact of video games on cognition; the pair eventually published the results of the study in *Nature*,[10] concluding that action video games helped to improve attention.

Bavelier was hooked. She wanted to find out the limits of video game–induced changes. She turned her attention to vision and contrast sensitivity (the ability to differentiate between subtle shades of the color gray) by conducting another study in which she found that people who played action games actually improved their ability to detect contrast and make sense of "visual clutter." For example, a driver with better contrast sensitivity finds it easier than others to identify the car directly ahead when there's fog on the road. To determine whether it's feasible to hone the same skills in a non-gamer, Bavelier asked a group of non-gamers to play action games for a few weeks, then sent them home, forbidding them to touch another game. Every few months, she'd ask them back to the lab to check their vision; she found that the positive effects of those short bursts of game playing were not wearing off. "We looked at the effect of playing action games on this visual skill of contrast sensitivity, and we've seen effects that last up to two years," Bavelier told National Public Radio in 2010.[11]

Taking things a step further, Bavelier partnered with UC Berkeley, McMaster University, and the school of interactive games and media at the Rochester Institute of Technology to see whether action games could be modified to help patients with amblyopia, or lazy eye. "There is evidence that certain computer-based activities—like reading—are more tiring for vision than others," Bavelier explained during a 2012 interview.[12] Reading forces the eyes to work over a very narrow range of spatial frequencies at high contrast, which can have an impact on vision different from the effects of playing video games, whose ranges tend to be much richer. "Clearly, it is not the monitor resolution itself, but what is actually on the screen and how you interact with it that is important for vision," Bavelier said.

Bavelier's work seemed to show that, though the brain's plasticity sags dramatically as we age, it is possible to curb the effects of this decline by stimulating the brain in the right way—in this case, through video games. Gazzaley was convinced. "I thought, yes, I can build a customized video game that specifically targets these deficits in the older adult brain, and see if the effects are passed on," Gazzaley says.

So he reached out to a few close friends who happened to work at LucasArts, the video game division of the now Disney-owned Lucasfilm. (LucasArts ceased operations in 2013.) The problem was that Gazzaley didn't know what kind of video game to make. A first-person shooter game in which players navigate different environments to kill enemies? A third-person adventure game that is more about puzzle solving and spatial awareness? Or a fast-paced action game, like the kind Bavelier had used? Gazzaley knew it needed to be something simple—because, after all, it was intended for an aging population—but he also wanted it to be engaging.

One night, he dreamt he was playing a driving game, but instead of racing against other drivers or avoiding barrels on the track, he was responding to differently colored signs. "I woke up and immediately sketched out some ideas in PhotoShop," he said. (Apparently, it's common for Gazzaley to dream solutions to problems he's working on.) He then sent the sketches to his LucasArts friends. The then-executive art director, Matt Omernick, introduced Gazzaley to one of the company's engineers, Eric Johnson, and a game designer named Noah Falstein, now the chief game designer at Google, who agreed to help Gazzaley build his driving game.

The team began meeting in Gazzaley's office and brainstorming design principles and goals over sushi and beer. Gazzaley began reading up on game design. The team spent months building a prototype of a game they called NeuroRacer, a 3D driving game similar to one a person might play at the DMV to qualify for a driver's license. In the game, the participant steers a car along a winding road using his or her left thumb. Every now and again, a sign pops up. If the participant recognizes the sign to be of a particular shape and color—something he or she has been instructed to watch out for—the object is to shoot it down using a finger on the right hand. These two tasks test cognitive skills like focus, multitasking, and working memory, which is the ability to temporarily retain multiple pieces of information. "[Both tasks] demand a lot of attention," Gazzaley said. "They are both getting harder as you get better. If you trade off one, the other one will suffer invariably. One of the rules of the game is that you only level up if you improve on both tasks, not just one."

That, of course, was the point. Gazzaley wanted participants' brains to figure out how to multitask without either task suffering. He regards cognitive-control abilities as kind of a triad of working memory, attention abilities, and goal management. NeuroRacer is an example of a goal-management challenge. Participants have two goals and must accomplish them both at the same time. There's no strategy or shortcut involved, and the key is not inherent skill. It's practice. The hypothesis was that if someone could get better at goal management, the person's attention abilities and working memory would also improve, because they involve similar parts of the brain.

The team began testing NeuroRacer on the thousands of volunteers who visited Gazzaley's lab for various studies. Finally, they recruited 180 adults between the ages of 20 and 70 for an in-lab study. The team found that older participants had a much harder time performing the multitasking activities than younger participants (an expected outcome). Next, 46 new volunteers aged 60 to 85 were asked to go home and play NeuroRacer for one hour a day, three days a week. After four weeks, the volunteers were tested again. On average, Gazzaley discovered that after playing the game as prescribed, the older participants fared much better in the multitasking requirement of the game (i.e., driving and reacting to signs at the same time) than both younger and older participants who had played NeuroRacer just once, as well as a control group that didn't play the game at all.

The study also found that those who had played NeuroRacer for a month at home fared better in tests of two other cognitive skills that involved areas of the brain that are similar to those responsible for multitasking but weren't directly exercised in NeuroRacer. The volunteers got better at responding to infrequent important stimuli and also improved their working memory— just as Gazzaley had predicted. More importantly, these skills did not deteriorate after six months, even without practice. (The game was accessible only via the laptops provided by the lab, which were taken away after the study concluded.) "It was shocking for us," Gazzaley recalled. "If we had known that was the case we would have tested much more than six months, but we just didn't expect it."

In September 2013, the results of the NeuroRacer study appeared on the cover of *Nature*.[13] "These [results] provide the evidence of how a custom-designed video game can be used to assess cognitive abilities across the lifespan, evaluate underlying neural mechanisms, and serve as a powerful tool for cognitive enhancement," Gazzaley concluded.

THE *NATURE* COVER BROUGHT Gazzaley and NeuroRacer a lot of attention. But Gazzaley didn't want people to assume that this was the holy grail of neurogames. He thought of it more as a blueprint for how one should marry the two fields. He also realized that he had to get NeuroRacer out of the lab and into people's hands. The game would need a serious update first; it had been created as an experimental prototype and not a commercial product. Gazzaley filed a patent for the methodology behind Neuro-Racer and set about trying to find someone who could help him turn it into a real game.

While attending a health and technology conference in Boston in 2011, Gazzaley had hit it off with a health industry entrepreneur named Eddie Martucci, who at the time was part of an investment start-up called PureTech. Martucci had come to the conference looking for inspiration. He wanted to form a company that could successfully combine neuroscience with entertainment software to create a new kind of medicine, one that could be both stimulating and effective. "Adam was giving his talk in the smallest conference room; it contrasted with the magnitude of what he was talking about," Martucci told us recently.

Martucci approached Gazzaley after his talk, and the two went for lunch. They spent the next four hours talking. Martucci didn't attend any other talks at the conference. A few months later, he invited Gazzaley back to Boston. "NeuroRacer immediately went on our shortlist of technology that we were looking for," Martucci said. Martucci had set a high bar for his future company: he wanted a solid platform with the right scientific pillars that could be built into software. He imagined something that could be both a video game and a medical device, with FDA approval, which doctors could prescribe to patients as readily as a drug. He knew it would take a lot of time and money to achieve this, not to mention exhaustive clinical trials.

The result, Akili Interactive, was incorporated in late 2011. Gazzaley later came on board as co-founder and chief science advisor. Martucci hired game designers and engineers, whose first task was rebuilding NeuroRacer into a consumer-grade action video game. The result, which took a year and a half, was a game called Project Evo. In this game, players have to guide an alien spacecraft through a canyon (instead of driving a car down a winding road). While steering, players must also click red-colored fish that appear intermittently on the screen, while ignoring green- and blue-colored fish. The game is self-sufficient: it doesn't need to be programmed by a doctor or clinician. Instead, it adapts naturally to each patient, increasing the speed of the ship and the speed and number of objects that the player must either click on or avoid.

The difficulty of the game changes to keep players at a certain success rate, i.e., that sweet spot where things are just starting to go wrong. The game also adapts second-by-second to give players incentive for pushing ahead. The goal of the game is to get players to become better at assessing sensory processing and interference processing at the same time. When the game senses a plateau—i.e., that a player has stopped making large gains—it reconfigures itself to be closer to the player's difficulty level. Akili calls Project Evo a "proprietary multitasking cognitive trainer." It's playable on mobile phones and tablets. "It's better [than NeuroRacer] in pretty much every way: art, music, story, better interactivity, more challenges, more user friendly, higher rewards, more accessible, and it's cloud-based," Gazzaley said. "It's just all the things we couldn't do in the lab."

Next, Martucci wanted to conduct a clinical trial for the game in exactly the same way a pharmaceutical company might conduct a new drug trial. The problem was that NeuroRacer wasn't built to target a particular "population," e.g., ADHD sufferers or Alzheimer's sufferers. Sensory processing seemed to be a problem in a lot of neurological conditions. Still, if Martucci wanted FDA approval, he'd need to make Project Evo's aims more specific. He spent nearly a year speaking to experts and mapping out the populations for which Project Evo could have the best effect. One of these was people with ADHD. Word of what Akili had in mind reached Shire, the pharmaceutical company behind Adderall, a leading ADHD prescription drug.

At the time, Shire was making equity investments in companies it wanted to work with in the future. Shire liked what Akili was proposing and invested in the company, partnering on a pilot study in 2013 that involved an ADHD-targeted version of Project Evo. (The results were released in October 2015 at the 62nd annual conference of the American Academy of Child and Adolescent Psychiatry.[14]) But how do you conduct a drug trial when the drug is a video game? Akili went through the same process as with a clinical drug trial, recruiting participants at four sites throughout the United States through online patient boards and doctor's offices. "Patients who want to participate come into the site, get a full workup of their symptoms, and instead of going home with a drug, they go home with an iPad." (In the recruitment process, Akili used the term "new medical device" rather than "video game," so as not to scare off parents.)

The subsequent trial involved 40 children between the ages of eight and 12 years in two groups: ADHD and "neurotypical"— a population that does not have whatever condition/disease is being studied. The kids were prescribed the game to play at home, on iPads, once a day over a period of four weeks. They were assessed clinically both before and after the study and were given a computerized assessment of attention, memory, and impulsivity. Parents were also asked to weigh in on their children's behavior before and after the study. After the trial, 11 of the 19 "outcome variables" in the computerized working memory test in the ADHD cohort showed significant improvement; parents also reported improvement in their children's working memory and inhibition, leading to the conclusion that the game "may be effective" in improving attention, working memory, and inhibition in pediatric ADHD population.

As importantly, the kids had a blast. "Although medication is the front line treatment for children with ADHD, there remains a need for the development of accessible, non-drug interventions," the subsequent report concluded. "Delivery of an effective intervention as an action video game on a mobile device may in the future provide an engaging way to treat ADHD symptoms in an at-home setting."

Pfizer then came knocking, wanting a similar drug trial for early-onset Alzheimer's. The company was specifically interested in Project Evo's data capture feature, which collects about 60 data points per second. Akili developed an Alzheimer's-specific version of Project Evo and, in partnership with Pfizer, plans to embark on a similar trial with people aged between 60 and 70 who have the neural markers for early-onset Alzheimer's. The goal is to test whether the game can identify those who are at risk for developing Alzheimer's down the track. Identifying those people, Martucci says, is something everyone in the pharmaceutical industry is currently trying to do.

Secondary platforms, games, and programs are already in the works, so that when Project Evo gets FDA approval—it no longer seems to be a question of *if*—there will be something in the pipeline. As with any new drug, FDA approval process is lengthy and involved. Akili is submitting Project Evo as a medical device, not a drug—similar to a hip implant or a new electrode. The company has sought FDA's feedback in past Project Evo clinical trials, and the response, according to Martucci, has been positive.

While the FDA cannot yet say a hard yes or no to whether the game will be approved, Martucci says the administration is "comfortable" with what Akili is doing. He expects the final approval to arrive before the end of 2017. Before that can happen, Akili has to do more to prove Project Evo's effectiveness among other populations. A larger, randomized control trial on ADHD has been planned, involving a few hundred patients across ten sites throughout the United States—a significantly larger group than in the first trial. Another trial, targeting autism, is also in the works. "We want a label that reads 'for the treatment of ADHD,' or 'for the treatment of X disorder,'" Martucci said. "For these claims, we need to get FDA approval for each patient population. And we will."

Later, in his lab, Gazzaley expressed a similar sentiment. "If five years from now doctors are pulling out prescription pads and writing, 'Four weeks of iPad training,' as opposed to a drug—that will be an incredibly exciting future."

GAZZALEY'S LAB AT UCSF resembles a doctor's clinic: pale blue walls, bright lights, and Purell dispensers in every corner. Here, a small research team conducts studies across a range of disciplines.

On a recent summer day, lab manager Cammie Rolle showed us inside one of the lab's testing rooms. On a large table in the corner sat a pile of what appeared to be blue, yellow, and red swimming caps, with a glut of thin white wires coming out of each one. "These are our EEG caps," Rolle explained. Participants wear the caps while playing a video game or engaging in other kinds of activity, and an EEG machine records brain wave activity.

Rolle fired up a computer screen with a visual test that some volunteers are required to do, in which they are shown increasingly violent and disturbing images, all while wearing an EEG cap. The point of the test, which is called an "emotional task," is to measure the increased levels of empathy in a participant's brain as he or she is reacting to each image. An image of a dead cat might yield a slight emotional response, while an image of a man with his head chopped off might yield a bigger one. The test begins with a set of neutral photos: a chair, a hairbrush, a shoelace. Then it's onto the provocative stuff. Participants' physiological responses—heart rate, blood pressure—are also measured.

After undergoing the emotional task, participants are asked to play a game on an iPad. A simple program asks participants to close their eyes for 30 seconds, then asks them if they were able to concentrate that whole time on keeping their eyes closed. If the answer is yes, the program increases the time a participant needs to close his or her eyes by a few seconds, and so on. The idea is that it's possible to train people to meditate.

Participants are allowed to take the iPads home for six weeks and must train five times a week. Then they must come back to the lab and redo the emotional task. The idea is that after participants learn to meditate, their responses to an image of a dead cat or decapitated head is not as strong. The heart rate isn't as high; they are simply more "chilled out," as Rolle says. The study is ongoing. Rolle recruits young adults through Craigslist and on different university campuses around town and pays them $15 per hour to participate.

Later, Rolle showed us the video game testing room, where the lab brings in participants involved in multitasking and distraction research studies, such as NeuroRacer. The lab's main focus is cognitive control, which can include everything from working memory to attention to multitasking to distraction. The video game room is certainly more fun than the lab rooms. Gazzaley wanted to build a space in which participants would feel comfortable—soft carpets, low lighting, a couple of couches, and two giant plasma televisions.

One television is used for an Oculus Rift–powered virtual reality demo in which participants can go inside the brain's neural networks and have a poke around. The brain in the demo isn't a computer-generated brain—it's someone's actual brain. "Let's say a person is about to go into brain surgery," Rolle explained. "A doctor can first fly through that person's brain and see what's going on."

The second television is reserved for Gazzaley's latest game, called Body Brain Trainer. Participants put on a heart rate monitor and stand in front of the screen while an Xbox One Kinect camera reads their body movements and tracks their positions. The idea is to measure, through a series of small tasks, how physical activity influences mental training. The first task determines each participant's fitness level, so the game can attune itself to each individual. Then, participants must play a series of increasingly difficult hand-eye coordination mini-games that utilize the Kinect's motion controls. The point is to test whether participants' ability to multitask in everyday life increases through practice. "Task switching is important and critical for our everyday functioning," Rolle said. "So by training that, we can actually see it has an applicable benefit." The study has been designed as an eight-week program, with participants coming in three times a week for an hour each.

Upstairs in Gazzaley's office, which looks like it could be Apartment Therapy's post of the week, Gazzaley spoke about the new game he's been working on called Rhythmicity, a rhythm training game. Grateful Dead drummer Mickey Hart is a collaborator. This time, the purpose is to improve people's rhythmic ability. "Rhythm is all about timing," Gazzaley explained. "The hypothesis is that if you are more rhythmic, perhaps there is transfer to other activities in life that require timing."

Gazzaley has slowly been learning the value of perfect timing since taking up nature photography in medical school when his uncle, a radiologist, gifted him a book by the photographer Galen Rowell. Gazzaley couldn't put it down. "I had just never thought about it as an artistic pursuit." He read the book cover-to-cover in the following eight hours. The next day, his uncle, amused, rummaged around the attic and brought down a Nikon camera from the year Gazzaley was born. "And he was like, 'This is your present!' I couldn't believe it." The uncle showed Gazzaley how to use the camera. The following week, Gazzaley took his first photo: a fiery Manhattan sunset. He developed the film and showed his friends. "And everyone was like, 'Wow, you're pretty good!' But I wasn't. I just got lucky." Gazzaley spent the next few months trying to take a picture as good as his first, without much luck. He reasoned that if he really wanted to be good at taking photos of nature, he'd have to experience some. So, in his final year of medical school, he went on a seven-week backpacking trip throughout New Zealand and Fiji. He came back with 70 rolls of film. "It changed my whole life," he later said. He got into the habit of printing his pictures at work. One night, one of the on-call nurses asked if she could buy one for her house. And then someone else said they wanted one too. Gazzaley started selling the prints for $20 a pop to hospital staff, and then, in 2000, launched an online business selling prints to hospitals and clinics. "Nature photography in the waiting room," he said. "You know, it relaxes people." He ordered an eight-foot-wide printer, and did his own framing. He had to give it up eventually when he came to San Francisco. (The business, not the photography.)

Every so often, he'll leave the lab and go on a photography expedition. He once spent two weeks walking and kayaking across Alaska, shooting 32 rolls of film. He sees photography and neuroscience as two sides of the same coin. "What I do in the lab and what I do with my camera—they're both an exploration of nature," he said. "Trying to understand it and find patterns in it. Trying to pull meaning from it."

He checked his Apple Watch. "Now, if you'll excuse me, I have another meeting."

PART IV

THE TOOLS OF A
NEW GENERATION

*Celebrating a New Breed of
Young Game Designers.*

9.

"Don't Just Buy a New Video Game—Make One!"

(PRESIDENT BARACK OBAMA, DECEMBER 8, 2013)

One chilly January morning, 25 eighth-graders sat on the floor of a classroom in a brick building in Manhattan's Chelsea district and began shouting at each other. They were playing a game called Socratic Smackdown, which calls for groups of four students to debate the meaning of a particular text in front of their peers. While they do so, the class keeps score: you get one point for agreeing with someone, one point for disagreeing with someone, two points each for agreeing/disagreeing and explaining why, and three points for using references from the text to support your argument. Anyone who cuts someone else off is docked two points. The text today was a poem—"The Hangman," by Maurice Ogden. A tall, blonde boy in the middle of the room was trying to make the case that the eponymous hangman was clearly supposed to symbolize death. Before he was done making his point, the girl next to him interrupted. "You're reading the text wrong," she said. Some of the students snickered. A student pointed out that he'd have to deduct two points because she'd interrupted. She shook her head. "I don't care. I can't sit here and listen to him talk about symbolism when he is so obviously wrong." The entire class cheered.

This is Quest to Learn, a public secondary school where the teaching curriculum is modeled on game design principles. Students in each class undertake a series of "missions" through the semester, broken up into smaller "quests." (Think of it as one large problem broken up into a series of smaller problems.) Missions and quests are designed by the school's teachers and are in line with state-set standards. The overall mission of the English class we visited was to write a dystopian story, which they titled "The Writer Games," after *The Hunger Games*. The teacher had been known to come to class dressed as Effie Trinket, the escort of the District 12 tributes in Suzanne Collins's novel and its sequels. That day's quest called for analyzing current dystopian fiction; hence Ogden's poem.

In another classroom, down the hall, sixth-graders were playing iCivics (remember Chapter 2?) on government-issued MacBooks. The teacher, a young woman with shiny black hair in a peach-colored power suit, said that this semester's mission was to pick a real Supreme Court case and have the class argue both sides, with three of their peers serving as "judges." Students would have the whole semester to prepare their cases, while the judges were tasked with reading up on the issue to ensure a fair and balanced decision. Last year's class had the same mission; the case they picked was *Obergefell v. Hodges*, the landmark 2015 case regarding marriage equality. "We nearly had a riot with that one," the teacher confessed. "The kids who were assigned to argue against it were incensed. They didn't understand how anyone could oppose a basic human right."

Classes at Quest to Learn also have unconventional names: "Sports for the Mind" stands in for media arts, and "The Way Things Work" is the rough equivalent of mathematics. In this semester's "Sports for the Mind," the students had to save New York from a fictional apocalypse by designing a role-playing game. Quests involved discussions of infrastructure and the different roles city officials play to keep a city safe during emergencies. (Hurricane Sandy provided ample real-world examples.) A floor below, kids in a fourth-grade class were designing their own superheroes on a complex-looking graphics program. "My superhero is a girl," a young boy with curly blond hair said, stepping aside so we could see his screen. "Because there aren't enough girls kicking butt."

A partnership between the learning design studio Institute of Play and the Department of Education in New York City, Quest to Learn opened in 2009 with funding from the MacArthur Foundation. The 650 students are spread across middle school and high school and are admitted by lottery. Classes are big, with around 30 kids each. The school shares building space with six other "experimental" schools; one is visual arts–focused, another is tech-focused.

High school students at Quest are given harder missions, and they "level up" faster than middle-schoolers. The gaming terminology also extends to grades—there are no A, B, or C grades at Quest. The school's equivalents are Novice, Apprentice, Senior, and Master. The idea is that those terms hold more meaning for the students, motivating them in a way that mere letters can't. Teachers work real-world elements into lessons whenever possible. One art and design mission involved energy-efficient food trucks. In ninth-grade biology, students spend the year as workers in a fictional biotech company, where their job is to clone dinosaurs and create stable ecosystems. As in many games, there's also a "boss level" mission. It usually takes place before the end of a semester and involves teams of about 15 students, with each undertaking a weeklong challenge. Last semester the challenge was to hold a fashion show with clothing made from recycled materials; before that, it was to create a functioning Rube Goldberg–inspired machine.

Quest to Learn students participate in the same standardized tests as the rest of the country; according to the Institute of Play, which commissioned a study from Florida State University into how well Quest students ranked among their peers, in the first 20 months, students at Quest showed significant gains in systems-thinking skills.[1]

Many people hear about Quest to Learn and think that students sit around playing video games all day. That's only partly true: digital game playing makes up around 20 percent of the curriculum. (There are also non-digital games and paper games.) The digital games usually have an educational bent, like Minecraft or Dr. Smallz, in which students take on the roles of designers, scientists, doctors, and detectives to explore cellular biology and the human body. Ninth-graders play Storyweavers, a collaborative role-playing game.

The appeal of the Quest to Learn curriculum is similar to that of a well-designed game: it requires participation and interaction, and there's immediate feedback. Challenge is a constant, and learning is achieved as much through failure as through success. Ross Flatt, a former assistant principal at Quest to Learn and one of its founding teachers, said that the kids who thrive at Quest are often the ones who don't mind making mistakes. Imagination and play are important, but the real keys are collaboration and a desire to be challenged in a way that sometimes isn't possible in other school environments. (The school has an advisory program for new students, to help them—and their parents—understand how the school operates. The program consists of sample missions and quests.) Teachers, too, need to be on board. "We look for teachers who are okay with letting go of absolute control," Flatt said. "Who can command respect while allowing the students to explore things beyond what's written down. And who don't mind going on tangents."

Flatt receives hundreds of requests every week from teachers and schools around the country who want to implement Quest to Learn's teaching model. Recently, representatives of a Chicago school asked for Quest's entire curriculum and tried to integrate it into their existing one. It didn't work out. The teachers were not given sufficient training, and students were often confused. "This is a concept that requires everyone to not just be on board and willing, but to actually understand why things are done in this way," Flatt said.

In recent years, forward-thinking educators like Flatt have helped build significant interest in the educational benefits of playing and designing video games. There is now increasing acceptance of the idea that the process of game making—the structuring of a world with constrained rules—enhances thinking and problem solving.

The idea continued to gain momentum with the announcement, in 2010, of the National STEM Video Game Challenge.[2] Launched by President Barack Obama at the White House, the challenge invited students across the country to design games that illuminated some aspect of science, technology, engineering, or mathematics. Launched in partnership with the Joan Ganz Cooney Center and E-Line Media, the challenge grew out of conversations during a number of gaming and learning summits held at the video game industry's annual trade event, the Electronic Entertainment Expo, known as E3, and organized by the Entertainment Software Association. The point of the challenge was to use the appeal of video games to encourage deeper learning about STEM topics, by both playing games and making them. By 2013, the challenge was receiving around 4,000 entries.

Mark DeLoura, a former senior advisor for digital media at the White House Office of Science and Technology Policy, watched it all happen. "The concept of the role at the White House was high-level: if we think games are a form of media that can have a broad societal impact, how can we encourage more development and utilization of these kinds of games?" DeLoura told us recently.

A self-taught programmer, DeLoura spent five years at Nintendo in tech support and another five years running developer relations at Sony PlayStation. He later headed up technology divisions at Ubisoft North America and the game publisher THQ. On the side, he wrote a series of books titled *Game Programming Gems,* designed to help aspiring programmers with tips and tricks from the best minds in game development. He made it to nine volumes before giving it up for the White House gig, for which he was put in charge of a team he dubbed the Federal Games Guild—its official name is much too long and boring to use in everyday conversation—and asked to seek out agencies and developers interested in working with the government to extend video games' application in classrooms around the country.

Slowly, DeLoura became Obama's go-to guy for tech and video game questions. He wrote the first draft of Obama's speech on the importance of learning to code. (The following year, Obama made headlines by becoming the first US president to write a computer program.) "It's easy to get cynical about government when you watch shows like *Scandal, The West Wing*, and *House of Cards*," DeLoura said. "But the reality is so much different. It was interesting to understand how the design of our government slows federal employees down so that if someone screws something up it doesn't break much, and this quality makes the wins you do get so much harder to achieve, and yet all that much sweeter when you do achieve them."

In 2014, DeLoura invited more than 100 game developers to the White House for the first game jam ever to be held inside the home of a US president.

Broadly, research suggests that adding a high-quality video game to a traditional educational curriculum can raise students' attention levels.[3] In 2014, a team of researchers reviewed existing studies on the psychological impact of playing video games[4] with a view toward countering the theory that playing violent video games is detrimental to mental health and behavior, especially in young adults. The review found that playing video games can actually strengthen cognitive skills, especially spatial navigation, reasoning, memory, and perception. "This has critical implications for education and career development, as previous research has established the power of spatial skills for achievement in science, technology, engineering and mathematics," concluded the lead author of the article, Isabela Granic of Radboud University Nijmegen, in the Netherlands. In a study published in 2013 and reviewed by Granic, the adolescents who reported playing strategic video games, such as role-playing games, also reported improved problem-solving skills and an improvement in overall grades in the following school year. Granic also found enough evidence in the studies they reviewed to suggest that games can be effective tools for teaching young children to build emotional resilience. All that failing and trying again has to be good for something.

In 2012, the website Onlinecollegecourses.com attempted something similar, combing existing research on the impact of video games in educational settings and coming up with a vibrant visual representation of the results:[5] an infographic that draws out the most relevant facts. Titled "Do Educational Video Games Actually Work?" the graphic cites one study that found that 18 percent of teachers in the United States use video games in class on a daily basis—but that K–5 teachers tend to use games more than middle school teachers (57 percent versus 38 percent). One study cited found that a staggering 95 percent of teachers use video games created specifically for educational use. Some 70 percent of teachers said games increased student engagement, while 60 percent said games helped them to better assess the students' skills and knowledge. A 2009 study cited also reported that students who play educational games are less likely to develop attention problems in school.

However, there's no hard data to show what kind of games have the most impact. This is one of the things DeLoura hoped to answer with the White House game jam. "We hoped to stimulate creation of a broad variety of educational game designs, and then test them to see which work best." So far, the argument goes something like this: Students who are *playing* a game are free to learn without the fear of making mistakes or getting bad grades. Students who are *making* a game automatically learn about a topic or concept in the process of trying to convey it effectively. Both are enormously effective approaches. "Games can be a fundamental component of keeping people excited about learning. It's almost a crime *not* to use them," DeLoura said.

But which is better: playing a game or making one? While playing games can make learning more engaging, teaching students to make their own games also means teaching them a skill—be it art, engineering, sound design, or production management. In an increasingly digitized world, not knowing how to write an Excel macro or a simple script to automate a task can leave one at a fundamental disadvantage. "I don't believe that every student needs to be a master programmer, but all should be exposed to programming and learn coding skills in school," DeLoura said.

This is the goal of Globaloria, a company that designs and runs video game–inspired courses for fourth- to 12th-grade classrooms in over 17 states. The point of the courses is to harness the appeal of games to inspire students to learn everything from coding and computer science to history, math, English, and science. "Learning is fun, but textbooks and lectures can be boring" is the company's oft-cited motto. At its heart, Globaloria is saying that creating, designing, and making a playable computer game or app is a much more successful way to teach and learn.

Globaloria courses ask students to come up with games or simulations related to particular topics—anything from mathematics to climate change to teen pregnancy. Students then work in teams to design the games and prototype them. Each Globaloria course is aligned with state and national standards and can be used by teachers as either a stand-alone curriculum or part of a larger module. According to the company, teachers and school librarians have used the courses to help teach advanced biology, principles of information technology, STEM, and game design and coding. Past student-made games have covered science, history, civics, and art. One game is about nuclear panic, another about the Spartans' war against the Persians. One game involves tracking down computer parts, while another entails helping Albert Einstein collect and combine atoms to create water. Still another game features jazz legends Louis Armstrong, Miles Davis, and Duke Ellington running away from an army of robots. "We're not teaching code simply to make coders as a vocation," Globaloria's founder and CEO, Dr. Idit Harel, said in 2014.[6] "When we say, 'coding is the new writing,' we mean that in every sense of how we use writing, from poetry to mathematics, from simple human communication to thought leadership."

Globaloria is also focused on attracting more girls to computer science. In 2012, Catherine Ashcraft from the National Center for Women and Information Technology (NCWIT) conducted a study of West Virginia classrooms that use Globaloria courses and found that female enrollment in Globaloria elective classes reached 33 percent in 2010–2011 and 37 percent in 2011–2012,[7] exceeding the national average for computing courses, in which female enrollment stands at around 20 to 25 percent. What's more, the girls who participated got more involved with computing activities at home, which helped them reevaluate the old trope that computers and games are just for boys. "I thought this class was only for boys," a middle school girl who participated in the study said. "I thought geeks only used computers, but then I really got to see the neat things about it. . . . It's not like boys get to do this or girls get to do this; it's whoever puts their mind to it, their heart to it, and their time, they can do anything."

Across the Atlantic, London-based Kuato Studios is using a different approach. Instead of creating games with testable curriculum content, the studio focuses on good design and storytelling, in the hope that students will learn coding skills without even realizing it. The studio was founded in 2012 with a proof-of-concept game titled Code Warriors, a strategic combat game that is set on an alien ship and involves a protagonist and giant robots. The catch is that players have to learn and use JavaScript to program their way out of hairy situations. No previous coding knowledge is required—the game simply guides the player along with a series of increasingly difficult challenges. Unlike a lot of educational games, Code Warriors was designed with tech-obsessed teens in mind: the game can be played on a desktop PC as well as a mobile phone or tablets. There's also Facebook integration, which encourages players to compete against friends and classmates.

David Miller, Kuato Studio's director of learning, and Mark Horneff, Kuato's managing director, took the game to schools around the UK and encouraged teachers to use it. To date, 600,000 hours of coding have been logged in the game—and that's just outside the classroom.

THE FUTURE OF VIDEO games will likely be shaped by a new generation of designers who grew up on a healthy diet of coding and game design principles—the kids at Quest to Learn, perhaps, or the young girls coding in a Globaloria class.

The self-taught developers of today's video game industry are proof of this. In the last ten years, independent games have blossomed into a market of their own. Now, anyone who can code and has a keen eye for story or visual flair can create and publish a game. Some games are made in a few days, or even a few hours. The one thing they have in common is that they aren't seeking mainstream approval or industry accolades; often, they are made to illuminate a moment or a feeling.

Crowd-funding platforms such as Kickstarter and Indiegogo have helped, as have services including Steam, which allows independent designers to publish their games without the backing of major games companies. Twine, a free, open-source platform that works with Mac, Windows, and Linux operating systems was specifically designed to allow anyone to make an interactive story, regardless of the person's coding skills. The tool publishes directly to HTML, meaning that users can put their games online instantly. Users can build passages of text and connect them with links. More experienced users can then layer different things on top: images, sound, CSS, JavaScript. Users can omit text entirely or simulate a whole world beneath it.

Twine was created by a web developer named Chris Klimas

in 2009. While in graduate school at the University of Baltimore's Interaction Design and Information Architecture program, Klimas began writing what he calls "hypertext fiction"—playing with interactivity and narrative outside a game. In order to make life easier for himself, he invented a set of tools that turned source code into interactive HTML. He showed them around to some friends, but no one seemed particularly interested, mostly because they were heavy on programming language and hard to comprehend.

At first, Klimas didn't think of Twine—the name he later gave to the program—as a game-making tool. It wasn't until he went public that he noticed that that's what the majority of people were using it for. Not that a lot of people *were* downloading it: maybe a total of 100 people actually used the first version of the program. But word spread quickly. Soon, independent developers were posting Twine games on their sites. Some were straightforward choose-your-own-adventure games. Others had complex, nonlinear storylines. In one, Queers in Love at the End of the World, two lovers have ten seconds left before the end of the world. The game is played in real time. Players can make the lovers hold hands, cry, talk, or fight. Each choice leads to a different outcome. When the timer hits zero, the game ends. Other games went the whole hog: sounds, pictures, music. One Twine game, called The Terror Aboard the Speedwell, is 50,000 words long.

There are now more than a hundred downloads of Twine per day. Klimas updated the software and moved it to a web-based platform. (The initial version required a download onto a PC.) Now, users can operate it straight from the website. There's even a tablet version. "I wanted people whose only access to computers is through a public library to have a chance to use it, and to meet halfway those whose primary experience with computers is a tablet," Klimas said.

Twine has certainly changed the way people think about games. It's given established game designers and enthusiasts a platform to challenge the notion that video games have to look and feel a certain way. Anna Anthropy, a celebrated game designer who helped spread the word about Twine, has been doing this for years. Her game Dys4ia, which is about gender identity disorder, has long been held as a leading example[8] of games' ability to explore marginalized issues with emotional depth.

Born in the Bronx, New York, Anthropy got into gaming through another DIY tool, shareware called ZZT. Like Twine, it didn't require previous programming knowledge. Anthropy was ten when she first started playing around with it; her dad was into gaming and had her hooked on Missile Command and Ms. Pac-Man. When her family bought a computer, Anthropy's first thought was to make her own games. She didn't know any programming, and at the time, there weren't a lot of resources for kids who wanted to learn it. All she had was a book about QBasic, a programming language, which proved to be a bad starting point. "It was totally incomprehensible," she told us recently.

One afternoon, she stumbled upon ZZT, an ANSI character-based video game made by legendary game designer Tim Sweeney in 1991. (Sweeney later founded Epic Games.) A DOS game, ZZT took place in text mode. Every graphic was composed of text characters—letters, numbers, playing card suites. (Hearts could represent health, for example.)

Anthropy eventually became infatuated with other things—drawing, comic books—and stopped playing around in ZZT. But she continued playing games. It wasn't until college that she stumbled upon a program called GameMaker. She was wary at first—it looked too technical—but her life circumstances soon became so turbulent that she turned to game design almost as a kind of therapy. She was attending university in New York, pursuing a dual major in creative writing and women's studies. But she didn't see a future in it, and she didn't want to be stuck in school forever. Plus, she'd had some bad experiences on campus. As a transgender woman, Anthropy had requested accommodations in the female dorms. But, she says, the university insisted that she needed to be in the male dorms. (She does not wish to name the university.) So she moved off campus, to White Plains, in Westchester County. The commute turned out to be long, and she couldn't keep up the rent payments. "I didn't feel like I was ever going to get my degree done, because I wasn't interested in my classes. I wasn't interested in academia in general." So she dropped out.

To take her mind off things, she began using GameMaker. Her first game was called Jay Walker. Players must run across the street at just the right moment to get as many cars as possible to crash into each other. Next, she tried something political: a shooting game called Kill Your Television, in which players shoot at television screens that play different advertisements. Anthropy enrolled in Southern Methodist University's Guildhall video game development program in Texas, but she didn't fit in there, either. "Their whole strategy was that they'd prepare you for the worst practices of the video game industry by making you go through them, one by one," she said. The work was tedious. One programming exercise called for students to create video game characters based on outdated clichés—ninjas, pirates, robots, monkeys, and so on. "They basically told me I could leave or get a better attitude. So I left."

In 2009, Anthropy returned to New York and began making Flash games, small, simple browser games made using Adobe Flash. Those had become something of a phenomenon around that time, and she earned money from companies like Adult Swim by making Flash games for their site. She accomplished her goal of earning enough to move to San Francisco, where a small community of independent game developers was forming and where she knew she'd find her niche.

She created Dys4ia in 2012. The game documents a six-month period in a transwoman's life, touching on every frustration, from taking drugs as part of the transitioning process to dealing with social prejudices. The game was small and basic, but it received international attention. Critics were impressed by its honesty and by Anthropy's ability to communicate the emotional underpinnings of such a personal, private experience so effectively.

Eventually, people began referring to Dys4ia as an "empathy game," a label that Anthropy is uncomfortable with. "You can't just play [Dys4ia] and suddenly know everything there is to know about being a transgender woman," she said. After Dys4ia was released, Anthropy began getting requests to exhibit the game at festivals. She was invited to speak at galleries specializing in interactive art. No one seemed particularly interested in her other work; they just wanted to know more about this game. So she stopped promoting the game and began charging a fee to show it in public. She once received an email from a curator in New York who was putting together an exhibition of empathy games at a gallery and wanted to exhibit Dys4ia. Anthropy told him she could not give her permission for the game to be displayed, but that she would send the gallery a pair of her old shoes instead. If people were so keen to learn what being a transwoman is like, they could literally walk in her shoes. She was kidding, but the curator loved it. She called the work *Empathy Game*—it consists of a pair of Anthropy's old boots on a podium, with a pedometer attached. There was also a chalkboard to keep score. The idea was that people put on the shoes to see how far they could walk. Most did not clear one mile. "The point is that you can walk for 20 miles or whatever and you would still not know what it's like to be me, to be a transwoman, or consider yourself educated on the topic," she said. "So why do you feel that way playing a five-minute game?"

The games Anthropy began making after she discovered Twine took off. And Twine took off along with them. Anthropy and Klimas met face-to-face for the first time at a conference two years ago. "It was emotional—we had steered each other's careers," Anthropy said.

Her next project is a children's book about DIY game creation, using free software like Twine. "The idea is that as long as you have a computer and an Internet connection, you can do everything." According to Anthropy, part of the problem with empathy games is that they try to reduce games to messages in order to teach or incite action, an approach that ignores the art of the form. She wants kids to grow up knowing how to make games the way she did, without necessarily needing a higher concept to aspire to.

"I want kids to grow up understanding games as just another art form," she says. "Not that they're better than comics or writing or whatever, but just another avenue to express what's going on with them. Games deserve that too—they deserve to be a thing people fill with the truth of themselves."

10.

Today and Tomorrow

(VIRTUAL REALITY AND A NEW BEGINNING)

One hot October morning in Palo Alto, California, a young man dressed in jeans and a short-sleeved shirt flew to the top of a building. He stood there for a brief moment, surveying the skyline, before diving and pulling up just short of a skyscraper. He floated in mid-air, turned around, and scanned the city below, seemingly searching for something. As he swerved between buildings and dived under bridges, he fumbled and lost his balance; suddenly, he veered into the side of a building and crashed into a pile of pixels.

This is Stanford University's Virtual Human Interaction Lab (VHIL), where researchers are studying the psychological and behavioral implications of virtual reality. On this particular morning, Shawnee Baughman, the lab's manager, was demonstrating one of the lab's 2013 studies, nicknamed "the superhero study."[1]

The aim was to test whether giving people superpowers, like fly-ing, in virtual reality encourages them to display more altruistic behaviors in real life. The lab tested 60 randomly selected par-ticipants for the original study—30 men and 30 women. To fly inside the virtual environment, subjects had to raise their arms above their heads, like Superman. To control speed, they could move their arms higher (to go faster) or lower (to slow down).

Part of the point of the experiment was to let subjects believe they were doing a great job. What participants didn't know was that a few minutes into the simulation, the figure at the center of their objective—a toddler in distress—was programmed to appear in the same spot at the same time, regardless of how well or poorly participants managed to fly inside the simulation. Next, a control group was put in the same virtual environment—except that this time, instead of controlling their own flight, they were simply passengers in a helicopter, also looking for the distressed toddler.

After each simulation, Baughman asked participants to sit down and answer a few questions. Halfway through the interview, she would pretend to knock over a cup of pens. She would then wait five seconds to see if participants rushed to help her pick them up or let her do it all herself. She would then begin collect-ing the pens—one pen per second. Participants who had played the superhero in the simulation were quicker to lend Baughman a hand, coming to her aid within three seconds. The helicopter sub-jects usually picked up the first pen, on average, after six seconds—one second after Baughman began picking them up herself. The superhero group also picked up around 15 percent more pens on average. And, while everyone in the superhero group picked up some pens, six participants in the helicopter group didn't offer to pick up any pens at all.

One of the study's conclusions was that video games could be used to encourage altruistic behavior. "If we can identify the mechanism that encourages empathy, then perhaps we can design technology and video games that people will enjoy and that will successfully promote altruistic behavior in the real world," Jeremy Bailenson, director of the VHIL, concluded at the time of the study.

The VHIL lab was constructed five years ago to study the link between empathy and virtual environments. The protocol for a VHIL study goes something like this: participants come in, fill out consent forms, and then step into one of the lab's two "treatment rooms"—kind of like a doctor's office, except fun. The rooms resemble a Hollywood recording studio: carpeted floor and walls and a giant screen on the back wall. Each has a *Minority Report*–style jumble of wires descending from the ceiling, attached to the Oculus Rift Development Kit 2 (DK2), the company's toolkit for developers in 2016. Prior to virtual reality headsets like the DK2, which is small and light, the lab used bulkier headsets usually made of metal. The one prior to the DK2 cost $40,000 (the DK2 cost $350).

Both rooms are equipped with infrared tracking systems. The largest room has cameras positioned along the top of the four walls, which pick up LED signals from the VR headset and additional LED markers attached to wristbands and ankle straps placed on participants. The cameras can track the position of the markers within less than one millimeter. The information is then beamed back to the computer in the next room, and the VR scene on the screen and inside the headset is rendered and redrawn many times per second in accordance with where participants are inside the space.

The sound system inside the lab is ambisonic, meaning that sounds come from a particular direction: up, down, left, right. There is also slight haptic feedback in the larger lab: 16 low-frequency subwoofers are hidden beneath the floor, which can make the ground of the lab shake a few millimeters. (The floor is made of airplane steel in order to carry the vibrations better.) In one of VHIL's earthquake demos, participants feel the floor beneath them shaking along with the VR simulation.

To get participants accustomed to virtual reality, Baughman usually runs the plank demo. This consists of a virtual environment that resembles the VHIL lab, where the objective is to walk from one end of the room to the other across a wooden plank. At some point in the demo, Baughman presses a button, and the floor beneath the plank gives way, creating the sudden sensation of being in the penultimate scene in *Indiana Jones and the Last Crusade*.

This kind of simulation can also be used to treat phobias—fears of anything from spiders to public speaking—through systematic desensitization. Imagine a weekly arachnophobia VR treatment in which you dunk your hand in a jar full of spiders and watch them crawl up your arm. (VR makes the experience slightly less terrifying than similar phobia treatments, which involve *actually* dunking your hand in a jar full of spiders in a controlled environment.) Another VHIL demo is designed to help train muscle memory. Participants stand in a virtual environment rendered to look like a warehouse stacked with boxes. The only other thing in the room is a long metal table. As the room begins to shake and boxes start to fall—the beginnings of an earthquake—participants' only obvious choice is to duck under the metal table. "Instead of just telling someone what to do, you can get them to perform an action in VR, and get them to retain the muscle memory for that action," Baughman said. In future, earthquake preparedness kits could come with VR training software.

The lab recently partnered with the Stanford football team to create a 360-degree video landscape of the field as it appears during practice. Members of the VHIL team attended and filmed weekly practices using a spherical camera and rig. The lab then stitched the different camera views together to create a virtual environment using the real footage. The aim of the study was to see if quarterbacks on the team could use VR to (1) make more accurate decisions on the field and (2) decrease their decision-making time on the field by reviewing the same plays over and over. The lab found that quarterbacks improved their decision making by 30 percent,[2] forming judgments and acting on the field a second quicker after having practiced in the VR environment. (One second may not sound like a lot, but every little bit helps when you're a quarterback.)

In July 2015, NFL commissioner Roger Goodell visited the VHIL to get a firsthand look at Bailenson's work. (He, too, was made to endure the plank demo.) During the visit, Bailenson and Goodell discussed other ways VR could enhance the football experience, for both players and fans. Those included re-creating sideline views and allowing fans to experience the same point of view as coaches and players; training both players and referees in a virtual environment; and the core of Bailenson's work—increasing empathy—which in this case meant allowing players to switch gender and race in a virtual environment to give them a peek into others' experiences, as well as to address domestic violence issues by putting players in the shoes of victims.[3] "That's unbelievable," Goodell was heard saying after taking off the DK2 headset in the lab.

One of the lab's biggest studies involved testing what's known as the Proteus effect, in which the aesthetic characteristics of a user's avatar can impact the user's behavior in a virtual environment. Bailenson created a series of virtual reality demos in which participants were given avatars of different ages, races, genders, levels of attractiveness, and so on, then monitored how participants behaved in both the virtual environment and in subsequent face-to-face interactions. In another study, the lab took a 3D model of each participant's face and then aged it with software, beaming it back into the demo when the participant faced him- or herself in the virtual mirror. According to Baughman, this particular study showed that participants who came face-to-face with their aged selves were more likely to delay gratification,[4] choosing to have rewards later rather than immediately. It was concluded that allowing people to interact with age-progressed renderings of themselves can cause them to allocate more resources to the future. (The Bank of America used the findings of the Stanford study as the basis for its Face Retirement program, which aims to motivate customers to invest more of their savings into retirement plans. According to the bank, more than one million customers have used the tool since it launched in 2012, with 60 percent choosing to learn more about the bank's retirement plans.[5])

The latest study at VHIL seeks to build on this work. According to the lab, previous empathy studies in VR have suffered from three shortcomings: first, small and homogeneous samples (typically upper-class college students), which limits researchers' abilities to draw conclusions across different cultures and communities; second, most studies fail to follow participants over time and therefore cannot determine the lasting effects of VR; and third, a limited range of empathy scenarios.

With new funding from the Robert Wood Johnson Foundation and in partnership with Dr. Jamil Zaki, founding director of Stanford's Social Neuroscience Laboratory, a new study will aim to collect data from a large, demographically diverse sample—approximately 1,000 participants—to test a wide range of empathy scenarios, from prejudice and bullying all the way to classroom learning.

IN THE LAST FEW years, virtual reality has evolved from a hobbyist's curiosity into the real deal. The 1990s VR craze suffered from a lack of accessibility: while the tech itself was improving, no one had yet managed to create a mass-produced piece of hardware at a price low enough to reach the average consumer. "[It] was a lot like the TV craze in the '20s—there was a lot of hype because it was exciting to think that such an amazing technology was possible," said game designer Jesse Schell, who scored his big break at the Disney Virtual Reality Studio in 1995 before becoming the studio's creative director. (He founded his own gaming company, Schell Games, in 2002.)

In recent years, new technologies like OLED displays and

more powerful rendering systems have made VR relevant again. Companies like Oculus VR, which began life as a Kickstarter campaign and went on to raise $2.4 million before being bought by Facebook for $400 million in cash and $1.6 billion in stock, are the vanguard. A consumer version of the Oculus Rift headset was officially released in March 2016 for $599. More companies have since joined the VR market—notably Sony, Microsoft, HTC, and Samsung—developing and releasing their own headsets and software. Google has a low-cost headset, Google Cardboard, for just $15. A user simply places a mobile device in the slot. The device works with a variety of apps. In May 2016, Google announced that Google Cardboard apps had reached 50 million downloads.[6]

"We have not previously had a medium that let us manipulate virtual objects with our hands in a direct and natural fashion," Schell said. While numerous studios and companies are working on VR films, documentaries, and video games, Schell believes most VR revenue and attention will stay focused on games, at least for the time being, because "that's where VR is at its strongest." Oculus VR has put its faith in John Carmack to lead this particular charge. Carmack, a video game industry legend, co-founded id Software and served as lead programmer on titles like Commander Keen, Wolfenstein 3D, Doom, and Quake, pioneering a handful of computer graphics techniques that went on to revolutionize 3D games.

A few years ago, Carmack became fascinated by Oculus co-founder Palmer Luckey's early Rift headset, making his own version using duct tape and writing code to run it.[7] Carmack's enthusiasm for tech sets him apart from other CEOs and company men. He'd rather spend an hour walking you through the back-end system of a gadget or the code of a particular piece of software than discuss stock prices or profit margins. His big plan for Oculus involves getting people excited about VR via mobile. "This is the job Oculus signed up for," Carmack told a roomful of video game developers in 2015. "It's almost a cliché when people say they want to serve a billion users with their product. But I do see a world in which a billion people use virtual reality headsets."

Carmack understands that people will want to take it slow at first, which is why he's come up with Gear VR, a head-mounted headset, powered by Oculus, that will work with Samsung mobile phones and run at 60 frames per second. Gear VR will have its own app store, for mobile VR experience on the go. Carmack thinks that at first, people will use it for simple things like looking at photos or videos. The hope is that they will rapidly begin to use the technology for longer, more immersive experiences like films and video games.

Oculus is headquartered in Building 18 on Facebook's sprawling campus in Menlo Park, California. Visitors enter through a drab-looking waiting area, kitted out with a few modest couches and a small fridge stocked with water and soft drinks. Beyond the large glass doors of the waiting room, the campus resembles Disneyland: manicured lawns, picnic tables, restaurants, food trucks, barbershops, newspaper stands, and ice cream stands, all populated with smiling, casually dressed employees who are either socializing or working on their laptops. Everything is free. (Alas, visitors are not allowed to walk around the campus unescorted.)

On a sunny October morning, we met with Laird Malamed, former Oculus COO and now the vice president and general manager of the Oculus Seattle team. Malamed is tall, with a mop of dark hair and soft features. He is another tech company executive with extensive experience in the games industry: the former senior vice president and head of development at Activision Blizzard, where he oversaw software, hardware, and manufacturing for blockbuster games like the Guitar Hero franchise, Call of Duty, and Skylanders. Malamed earned a joint degree in aeronautical and astronautical engineering and film and media studies at MIT, later attending the Graduate School of Cinematic Arts at the University of Southern California (USC).

After an internal reshuffle at Activision in 2004, Malamed took over a lot of the kids' franchises that nobody seemed to want. As a parent, he'd watched his son play "edutainment" games that neither looked nor played particularly well. So he teamed up with his wife, a physician, to start an educational consulting company, which led him to do some work with his alma mater, USC. "That really opened up my eyes to the potential for interactivity in teaching," he told us.

While still at Activision, Malamed and USC collaborated on a concept for a civics game that would teach American constitutional history to high school students. Players could choose either to be "forces of change" or the "status quo" in a debate over constitutional issues. The idea was that students could toggle the Bill of Rights on and off, replaying the same scenario in different versions of the same world; for example, with freedom of speech toggled off, the game would show students just what it would mean to live in a world without that basic right. "We were looking for standard experiences, so that we could point out where our civil liberties are so prevalent you almost do not notice them,"

Malamed said. In one proposed scenario, a teacher might be talking to her students about evolution and creation. But with religious freedom turned off, the principal might come in and fire her for discussing religious subjects in school. Later, the scenario might switch to a peaceful demonstration. With the right to assembly turned off, police might arrest everyone. However, USC's educational partners argued that it was too much to expect of students to understand the difference between a real world and a false one. "They were worried students would end up liking the 'bad' version of the world, in which you could kill and maim and do all that stuff without retribution, better than the 'good' version of the world, where the Bill of Rights existed," Malamad recalled.

By 2011, Malamed, who was now teaching at USC, decided to leave Activision to focus on education. He spent a year working on various projects, including one, with the Bill and Melinda Gates Foundation, called the Radix Endeavor—an educational massive multiplayer online game (MMO) for middle and high school students that targets STEM learning outcomes. Then, in 2012, one of Malamed's students at USC showed him a Kickstarter campaign for a virtual reality headset called Oculus Rift. Intrigued, Malamed tried one of the early prototypes of the headset. "My first reaction was that it was pretty bad, but it showed promise." What he liked about it was that, from a start-up point of view, it wasn't hard to describe the benefit of the headset—it allowed you to do basically anything, anytime, anywhere, with anybody. People didn't have to have a technology background, or be familiar with *Star Trek*, to appreciate what that meant. (For the non-Trekkies: the world of *Star Trek* includes a virtual reality system called the holodeck, which renders different environments in virtual reality, allowing characters to revisit certain places or hone particular combat or sporting skills.) A former colleague introduced Malamed to the Oculus VR team, which had about seven employees at the time. "They were looking for someone to help run operations, and who had experience with both hardware and software, and with a background in games. I ticked all those boxes," Malamed said.

He started working at Oculus in 2013. While the company's primary goal is entertainment, it has kept the platform open, inviting anyone who has an interest in virtual reality to build experiences for the Rift headset (an opportunity that Stanford's VHIL is embracing wholeheartedly). The company's research team in Redmond, Washington, is also investigating potential long-term uses of virtual reality, in partnership with neuroscientists, universities, and VR labs around the world. "We're seeing a lot of single person [VR] activities now because we're at the beginning, and that's what's technically possible right now, but that will change," Malamed said. "We don't go on vacation on our own, so why would you go into VR on your own? Eventually, people are going to want to share that experience with others."

OTHERS SHARE MALAMAD'S VIEW of a future in which virtual reality is inextricably linked to our social interactions. In 2012, a group of graduate students from Barcelona devised an art installation in which audience members could enter a stranger's body using virtual reality. The work, titled *Machine to Be Another*, was designed to promote empathy and eliminate gender and race bias. During a four-month residency at the L'estruch Cultural

Center, in Spain, the group, known as Be Another Lab, devised a series of experiments using two head-mounted goggle displays running the latest version of Oculus Rift, the virtual reality headset, and two cameras transmitting a real-time video feed of each participant's point of view. During the experiment, known as the Gender Swap, participant A sees what participant B is looking at, and vice versa.[8] So if one participant is male and the other female, each views the other's body as his or her own. "Almost always, the guy will say, 'Oh yeah, I've been wondering what it's like to be a girl all my life,' and the girl usually is taken aback by this," Philippe Bertrand, a member of Be Another Lab, told us recently. "She usually says, 'I have never wondered what it's like to be a guy.'" The team expected that during initial Gender Swap performances, men would do the stereotypically male thing and try to touch their partners' bodies, but that rarely happened. "One thing people don't understand until they do this is that you need constant consent and agreement. It feels like you're in someone else's body, but you can't really treat it as if it's your own. There's a constant negotiation of personal space. And it flips: their personal space becomes yours, and you're suddenly protective of it." As a result, people, especially men, tend to be more conservative than they originally intended to be. "It ends up being about mutual respect," Bertrand said. "It's hard to teach that to someone until they've actually experienced what it's like to be in the other person's body."

Sometimes, audience members are not allowed to see the people they're swapping bodies with until the performance begins. "You enter a space and you don't see who is on the other side and suddenly you're inside someone else's body, looking at their face, hands, and their body," according to Bertrand. Over time, the performances became more elaborate. In one version, audience members swap bodies with a performer who recounts a personal story while interacting with different objects: a childhood photo, a pack of cigarettes, a handheld mirror. In another version, called the Age Swap, audience members are paired with performers or other audience members much older or younger than themselves. There's even a naked version, for those bold enough. "We did the naked version once with two guys—one in his twenties and the other in his fifties," Bertrand said. "They had some kind of spiritual awakening: the older guy saw himself as a younger man, and the younger guy saw himself grow old. They were both completely overwhelmed when they came out of the room."

After releasing a video of the Gender Swap experiment, Be Another Lab received invitations from around the world, sent by universities and cultural institutions interested in using *Machine to Be Another* to study conflict resolution, rehabilitation, and body dysmorphia. New performances were devised; in one, audience members are paired with a former Iraqi soldier, who shares her memories and experiences of war. In another, designed to study pain tolerance, participants are asked to keep their hands in a bowl of freezing water for as long as possible—once while staring at a blank wall, and again while using the *Machine to Be Another*. Bertrand says that participants are usually able to keep their hands submerged for at least twice as long while using the *Machine*, because, essentially, it distracts them from the pain.

More recently, Be Another Lab has collaborated with the Museum of Contemporary Art in Barcelona, the Institute of the Future in San Francisco, Pace University in New York, the University of Denmark, and the United Nations, for which the group, in collaboration with Somali storytellers, devised a performance surrounding conflict resolution. The team was also invited to demonstrate *Machine to Be Another* at an MIT workshop investigating neurorehabilitation. "Understanding someone else's point of view has the potential to have an impact on every aspect of everyday life," Bertrand says.

The next step is to make *Machine to Be Another* accessible to anyone who wants to use it for noncommercial purposes. The physical components—Oculus Rift, cameras, and microphones—can be bought online. "We try and use off-the-shelf components, stuff that's easy to make at home so anyone can do it," team member Christian Cherene says.

IF SCHELL IS RIGHT, and video games will be largely responsible for driving the VR juggernaut forward, at least for the time being, then a large part of the immediate innovation will fall on game designers. While large video game studios have already begun taking cautious steps in this direction, it's really the small guys—independent designers and those at studios with little to lose—who have embraced the challenge of building a new medium from the ground up with the same gutsiness that has defined the independent games movement. Take Ustwo, for example. The digital design and development company has offices in the United Kingdom, Sweden, the United States, and Australia and, although the majority of their work is client-focused, dedicates some 10 percent of its profits to developing proprietary projects.

In 2014, Ustwo launched a mobile and tablet puzzle game

called Monument Valley. The game's distinctive art style mirrors the calculated beauty of a Japanese print, or, better yet, the brain-melting elegance of an Escher drawing. The game was a hit; it won Apple's 2014 Design Award and was named the iPad Game of the Year, among a handful of game industry nods. It went on to sell more than two million copies. (More auspiciously, Frank Underwood played it on *House of Cards*.) Dan Gray, the head of Ustwo's gaming division, is just 30 years old. He joined Ustwo after stints at Lionhead Studios, where he worked on the Fable franchise, and Hello Games, where he worked on the Joe Danger series. (Hello Games went on to create No Man's Sky, the procedurally generated open-world game that features some 18 quintillion planets for players to explore.) "When I met the guys at Ustwo it was just so different to the basements filled with middle-class white guys I was used to," Gray told us recently. "I just knew that we could create something different." According to Gray, the motivation behind Monument Valley was to create "the perfect iPad game." "We like to think of it as a coffee table book of a game that people replay for the artistic adventure and show off to friends when they get the chance."

After he had worked on Monument Valley for 18 months, Gray's attention turned toward VR. Where other studios might have followed the money and produced a sequel, Gray had seen enough first-person shooter and tower defense games in virtual reality to know that there were still plenty of opportunities to do something truly innovative in the new medium—something that didn't involve explaining 20 different button layouts to users. The result was Land's End, a VR game for the Samsung Gear VR headset.

The game is, in some ways, similar to Monument Valley: it's filled with the same dreamy landscapes and elegant puzzles. However, the way players solve puzzles has changed somewhat: in Land's End, all players have to do is *look* at something to interact with it. The same goes for moving from location to location. Players move by looking in the direction they want to go. Because of this, the game is accessible to anyone, regardless of their gaming skill level or their familiarity with virtual reality. The game was released in November 2015. Its simplicity instantly set it apart from other virtual reality games. Instead of being overwhelming, the game was intuitive—and beautiful. And, perhaps best of all, no one got sick while playing it. "In the same way you can give Monument Valley to your grandparents on an iPad and have them enjoy themselves, we wanted to create a VR experience that didn't need an introduction—it could just be enjoyed," Gray said.

ACCORDING TO SCHELL, VIRTUAL reality experiences like Land's End will soon trump day-to-day reality as the technology catches up. Eye tracking, voice tracking, body tracking, and augmented reality—all VR experiences will master the basics. Virtual reality will become so technically and artistically proficient that it might just one-up face-to-face interaction.

"A good way to think of 2016 is kind of like 1978," Schell said. "In 1978, home computers like the Atari 800 appeared in stores. People criticized them—too expensive, and who needs a computer anyway? But the entertainment experiences they provided were powerful, and a whole digital revolution began. We are going to see something similar with virtual reality. And just as it happened with computing, new uses are going to appear that we haven't even thought of yet."

Power Playlist

DISCOVER SOME OF THE GAMES (AND GAME MAKING TOOLS)
MENTIONED IN THE BOOK

CHAPTER ONE: A LITTLE GAME ABOUT PEACE

PeaceMaker (2007)—http://www.peacemakergame.com/
September 12 (2003)—http://www.newsgaming.com/games/index12.htm

CHAPTER TWO: A FORMER SUPREME COURT JUDGE
TAKES MATTERS INTO HER OWN HANDS

Do I Have a Right?—https://www.icivics.org/games/do-i-have-right
Executive Command—https://www.icivics.org/games/executive-command
Win the White House—https://www.icivics.org/games/win-white-house
Branches of Power—https://www.icivics.org/games/branches-power

CHAPTER FOUR: A PRINCE'S TALE

The Cat and the Coup—http://www.thecatandthecoup.com/

CHAPTER SIX: A LAB OF HOPE

Remission 2—http://www.re-mission2.org/games/

CHAPTER SEVEN: ARMCHAIR SCIENTISTS

Foldit—https://fold.it/portal/
Nanocrafter—http://nanocrafter.org/game
Zooniverse—https://www.zooniverse.org/projects
Lab in the Wild—http://www.labinthewild.org/

CHAPTER EIGHT: UNDER THE HOOD

Throw Trucks with Your Mind—http://crooked-tree-studios.myshopify.com
    /collections/all
Project Evo (sign up for the trial)—http://www.akiliinteractive.com/#contact
    -section

CHAPTER NINE: "DON'T JUST BUY A NEW VIDEO GAME—MAKE ONE!"

Code Warriors—https://play.google.com/store/apps/details?id=com
    .kuatostudios.hakitzu&hl=en
Twine—https://twinery.org/
GameMaker—http://www.yoyogames.com/gamemaker
Dys4ia—https://w.itch.io/dys4ia

CHAPTER TEN: TODAY AND TOMORROW

Monument Valley—https://play.google.com/store/apps/details?id=com.ustwo
    .monumentvalley&hl=en
Land's End (VR)—http://www.landsendgame.com/

Acknowledgments

Beyond this book there is an ever-growing movement, and I would like to thank and acknowledge the contribution of many who helped create its momentum, who gave me and many others opportunities along the way, and who collaborated or inspired me.

Let me begin with the co-founders of Games for Change (G4C)—Suzanne Seggerman, Barry Joseph, and Benjamin Stokes—and the visionary first funder who supported them, Dave Rejeski of the Woodrow Wilson Center. Special thanks go to Michelle Byrd, who co-led the organization with me for three years (2010–2013), and Alan Gershenfeld, former chairman of the G4C board, who mentored me and created this opportunity in the first place.

I wish all the best to Susanna Pollack, my successor as president of G4C, who is always a true collaborator. The G4C team is incredible, dedicating their time and work for a purpose: Sara Cornish, Kevin Duggan, Tania Hack, Emily Treat, Meghan Ventura, Hsing Wei, and Victoria Abrash, who has since departed. My friends Raanan Gabriel (design) and Yair Avgar (technology) were always there to help me with advice, goodwill, and excellent work.

Jean Michel Blottiere and Gilson Schwartz pushed the movement in Europe and Latin America respectively, often against all odds.

G4C has a terrific board that was led for many years by Ken Weber. Ken was also one of the greatest friends of the sector and of myself, and the reason G4C made it through turbulent times. Jane McGonigal always inspired me with her boldness and leadership. David Sharrow and Charles Glass were both very generous with pro bono legal support. Erik Huey and Michael Gallagher of the Electronic Software Association have been true supporters of games for good and learning. Other leaders and thinkers in the space always inspired or challenged me, among them: Beth Bryant, Brian Crecente, Mark DeLoura, Mary Flanagan, Tracy Fullerton, Idit Harel, Michael Levine, Colleen Macklin, Matt Parker, Susana Ruiz, Ben Sawyer, Constance Steinkuehler, Greg Trefry, and Eric Zimmerman.

A few funders and partners showed incredible leadership and hinted at what's possible: Connie Yowell at MacArthur, Maryanne Yerkes at USAID, Alyce Myatt at NEA, and Kathy Reich at Packard. The team at Tribeca Enterprises is helping take G4C to new heights with our partnership: Jane Rosenthal, Craig Hatkoff, Jon Patricof, Casey Baltes, Pete Torres, Paul Downing, Patty Newburger, Nancy Lefkowitz, and many on their staff. Cheryl Heller, the founder of the Social Innovation program at SVA, was the first to realize that G4C could also be a great academic course. We've been teaching it for four years. Chelsea Stark made the G4C Awards accessible to millions through Mashable, and Geoff Keighley made it a category in his Game Awards.

Carnegie Mellon, and specifically the Entertainment Technology Center, is where PeaceMaker was born, thanks to the unique program designed by Don Marinelli and the late Randy Pausch. Other forces on the faculty were always there to lend advice and support: Steve Audia, Tina Blaine, Drew Davidson, Brenda Harger, Chris Klug, Charles Palmer, Jesse Schell, Ralph Vituccio, and Josh Yelon. Special thanks to Shanna Tellerman and Brian Schrank, who joined the original student team comprised of Eric Brown, Eric Keylor, Olive Lin, Ross Popoff, Tim Sweeney, and Victoria Webb.

Eric Brown had a huge part as my first partner in the United States; I learned so much from him and couldn't have done any of it without him. Jared Cohon, then president of CMU, has been incredibly accessible, and the Pittsburgh investor community—Michael Matesic (Idea Foundry), Innovation Works, and the angel investor Bill Recker—all helped us fly out of CMU and into the real world. When times got rough, my parents, Ada and Jacob, together with Hezzi Ker and Calvin Mew, gave us financial and emotional support to keep us going.

On the Half the Sky Movement, I owe thanks to Maro Chermayeff's team at Show of Force, with whom we created a true cross-media partnership: Josh Bennet, Jeff Dupre, Andrew Hall, Liriel Higa, Rachel Koteen, and Melle Patrick. The list of funders and supporters of the project is too long to include here, but the Zynga team stands out and lifted us up: Emily Anadu, Rob Aseron, Virginia McArthur, and, of course, Abby Speight. On the creative side, the team at Frima took a risk: Marie-Helene Bellemare, Steve Couture, and Pierre Moisan; the Mudlark team worked under extreme constraints: Charles Hunter and Matt Watkins; the ZMQ team made sure we keep it real: Subhi and Hilmi Quraishi; and the social media and outreach were led by the dedicated Soraya Darabi, Lisa Pastor, and Ashley Alicea.

Rhalee Hughes introduced me to my book agent, Anthony Mattero, from Foundry, who always believed in us and had great insight at every turn. The publishing team at Macmillan/ St. Martin's Press has always been on the mark, so thanks to Emily Carleton and Alan Bradshaw. Thanks to the team at Sunshine Sachs—Damiano DeMonte, Jason Lee, and Jaclyn Rutigliano.

The ones who read the first draft and shared meaningful feedback were my father, Jacob, Yuval Sheer, and Bruce Hack. Greg Toppo, the author of *The Game Believes in You*, gave us some great pointers at the beginning of the journey.

My wife, Britta, and my family, who always displayed great patience and understanding, and I can't thank them enough.

—Asi Burak

Notes

chapter 1

1. Israel Channel 2, uploaded March 26, 2007, https://www.youtube.com /watch?v=R66qqIj8nQo.
2. Randy Pausch, "Last Lecture: Achieving Your Childhood Dreams," uploaded December 20, 2007, https://www.youtube.com/watch?v=ji5 _MqicxSo.
3. Gonzalo Frasca, "September 12th: A Toy World," 2003, http://www .gamesforchange.org/play/september-12th-a-toy-world/.
4. Fahdi Mansour, Al-Jazeera (Arabic), April 23, 2007, https://www .youtube.com/watch?v=34RBplTHnLQ.
5. Clive Thompson, "Saving the World, One Video Game at a Time," *New York Times*, July 23, 2006, http://query.nytimes.com/gst/abstract.html ?res=9901E3DB163FF930A15754C0A9609C8B63.
6. Peres Center for Peace, "PeaceMaker," http://www.peres-center.org /peacemaker.
7. Cleotilde Gonzalez, Ronit Kampf, and Jolie M. Martin, "Action Diversity in a Simulation of the Israeli–Palestinian Conflict," *Computers in Human Behavior* 28(1), January 2012: 233–240.

chapter 2

1. Games for Change, "Opening Keynote—The Honorable Justice Sandra Day O'Connor," uploaded July 23, 2010, https://vimeo.com/13579793.
2. Seth Schiesel, "Former Justice Promotes Web-Based Civics Lessons," *New York Times,* June 9, 2008, http://www.nytimes.com/2008/06/09 /arts/09sand.html?_r=2.
3. Sandra Day O'Connor Institute, "Sandra Day O'Connor Biography," uploaded 2012, http://www.oconnorhouse.org/oconnor/biography.php.
4. James Paul Gee, *What Video Games Have to Teach Us about Learning and Literacy* (New York: Palgrave Macmillan, 2007).
5. Bob Salsberg, "Geography Comes Alive with Carmen Sandiego," *Kentucky New Era,* January 27, 1992, https://news.google.com/newspapers ?id=fd0rAAAAIBAJ&sjid=VGQFAAAAIBAJ&dq=carmen-sandiego &pg=5934,2297264&hl=en.
6. Debra Cassens Weiss, "O'Connor Corrects Jon Stewart in *Daily Show* Appearance (See the Video Clips)," *ABA Journal,* March 4, 2009, http:// www.abajournal.com/news/article/oconnor_corrects_jon_stewart_in _unusual_comedy_central_appearance.
7. The National Constitution Center, "More Teens Can Name Three Stooges Than Can Name Three Branches of Government," September 2, 1998, http://constitutioncenter.org/media/files/survey-1999-stooges.pdf.
8. The Civic Mission of Schools, "Guardian of Democracy: The Civic Mission of Schools," 2011, http://civicmission.s3.amazonaws.com/118 /f0/5/171/1/Guardian-of-Democracy-report.pdf.
9. Anthony Lutkus and Andrew R. Weiss, "The Nation's Report Card: Civics 2006," National Assessment of Educational Progress, May 2007, http://nces.ed.gov/nationsreportcard/pubs/main2006/2007476.asp.
10. iCivics, "Our Impact," retrieved 2016, https://www.icivics.org/our-story.
11. Persephone Group, "Evaluation of iCivics Games: Executive Summary," October 2009, https://www.icivics.org/our-story.

chapter 3

1. Rajini Vaidyanathan, "Why Don't Black and White Americans Live Together?" *BBC News,* January 8, 2016, http://www.bbc.com/news/world -us-canada-35255835.
2. William H. Frey, "Census Shows Modest Declines in Black-White Segrega-

tion," Brookings Institute, December 8, 2015, http://www.brookings.edu
/blogs/the-avenue/posts/2015/12/08-census-black-white-segregation-frey.

3. Network Impact, "Macon Money Game Evaluation: Summary Results,"
March 3, 2012. (Not published online.) Part of the results online at:
http://www.knightfoundation.org/media/uploads/publication_pdfs
/Knight_Games_Evaluation_Brochure.pdf.

chapter 4

1. Clyde Hughes, "Saudi Prince Disneyland Adventure Cost Him and
Friends $19M," *Newsmax.com*, June 5, 2013, http://www.newsmax.com
/TheWire/saudi-prince-disneyland-adventure/2013/06/05/id/508104
/#ixzz49aiDW6Dc.

2. Bhagwandas, "Arab Royal Hunts Down 2,100 Houbara Bustards in
Three Week Safari," *Dawn*, April 22, 2014, http://www.dawn.com/news
/1101272/arab-royal-hunts-down-2100-houbara-bustards-in-three
-week-safari.

3. *Le Mag* with AFP, "Disneyland Paris Privatized for Three Days at 15
Million Euros a Saudi Prince," June 3, 2013, http://www.lemag.ma/Le
-Disneyland-Paris-privatise-pour-trois-jours-a-15-millions-d-euros
-pour-un-prince-saoudien_a71831.html.

4. Stanford University, "Sigma Nu Fraternity," 2010, http://web.stanford
.edu/group/sigmanu/history.php.

5. Saudi Arabia Demographics Profile, Index Mundi, 2014, http://www
.indexmundi.com/saudi_arabia/demographics_profile.html.

6. Ian Black, Jemima Kiss, "Facebook Launches Arabic Version," *Guardian*,
March 10, 2009, http://www.theguardian.com/media/2009/mar/10
/facebook-launches-arabic-version.

7. Woodrow Wilson International Center for Scholars, "Saudi Arabia's Youth
and the Kingdom's Future," Middle East Program PDF, 2011, https://www
.wilsoncenter.org/sites/default/files/Saudi%20Arabia%E2%80%99s
%20Youth%20and%20the%20Kingdom%E2%80%99s%20Future%20
FINAL.pdf.

8. Debra L. Oswald, "Understanding Anti-Arab Reactions Post-9/11: The
Role of Threats, Social Categories, and Personal Ideologies," *Journal of
Applied Social Psychology* 35 (September 2005): 1775–1799.

9. Shubh Mathur, "Surviving the Dragnet: 'Special Interest' Detainees in
the US after 9/11," *Race and Class* 47 (January 2006): 31–46.

10. Martin Jay, "FBI Surrounds House of Saudi Student after Sightings of Him with Pressure Cooker Pot—Only to Discover He Was Cooking RICE," *Daily Mail*, May 12, 2013, http://www.dailymail.co.uk/news/article -2323316/FBI-surrounds-house-Saudi-student-following-sightings -pressure-cooker-pot-cooking-rice.html#ixzz49bSlVeLe.

11. Statista, "Percentage of Internet Users in the Total Population in Selected Countries of the Middle East in 2014," 2014, http://www.statista .com/statistics/265836/internet-penetration-in-middle-eastern -countries/.

12. Freedom House, "Freedom on the Net 2012," 2012, https://www .freedomhouse.org/sites/default/files/Saudi%20Arabia%202012.pdf.

13. Maya Rahal, "Quick Stats about Internet Usage in the Middle East," *Wamda*, March 27, 2013, http://www.wamda.com/2013/03/13-stats-about -internet-usage-in-the-middle-east.

14. Arab Social Media Report, "Twitter in the Arab Region," March 2012, http://www.arabsocialmediareport.com/Twitter/LineChart.aspx? &PriMenuID=18&CatID=25&mnu=Cat.

15. Ben Hubbard, "Young Saudis See Cushy Jobs Vanish Along with Nation's Oil Wealth," *New York Times*, February 16, 2016, http://www .nytimes.com/2016/02/17/world/middleeast/young-saudis-see-cushy -jobs-vanish-along-with-nations-oil-wealth.html.

16. Maya Rahal, "What You Should Know about Amman's Tech Sector [Infographic]," May 20, 2014, http://www.wamda.com/2014/05/amman -regional-technology-capital-startups.

17. The Embassy of the Hashemite Kingdom of Jordan, Washington, DC, "Remarks by His Majesty King Abdullah II at 'Innovative Jordan' Conference in University of California at Berkeley," 2014, http://jordan embassyus.org/news/remarks-his-majesty-king-abdullah-ii-innovative -jordan-conference-university-california.

18. Staff and agencies, "Dozens of Saudi Arabian Women Drive Cars on Day of Protest against Ban," *Guardian*, October 26, 2013, http://www.theguardian .com/world/2013/oct/26/saudi-arabia-woman-driving-car-ban.

19. Katherine Zoepf, "Shopgirls," *New Yorker*, December 23, 2013, http:// www.newyorker.com/magazine/2013/12/23/shopgirls.

20. Vivian Nereim and Donna Abu-Nassr, "Saudi Women Are Joining the Workforce in Record Numbers," *Bloomberg*, August 10, 2015, http:// www.bloomberg.com/news/articles/2015-08-10/saudi-women-are -joining-the-workforce-in-record-numbers.

21. "Women in Saudi Arabia to Vote and Run in Elections," *BBC*, September 25, 2011, http://www.bbc.com/news/world-us-canada-15052030.

22. "Three Consecutive Declarations for Divorce Should Be Punishable Offence: CII," *Dawn.com*, January 21, 2015, http://www.dawn.com/news /1158471.

23. "Saudi Arabia's Women Vote in Election for First Time," *BBC*, December 12, 2015, http://www.bbc.com/news/world-middle-east-35075702.

24. Hugh Miles, "Saudi Arabian Divorced Women and Widows to Get Greater Legal Powers," *Guardian*, December 2, 2015, http://www.the guardian.com/world/2015/dec/02/saudi-arabian-divorced-women-and -widows-to-get-greater-legal-powers.

chapter 5

1. Mudlark Studio, "9 Minutes," uploaded January 7, 2013, https://vimeo .com/56911873.

2. Half the Sky Movement, "Launching Half the Sky Movement Games in Kenya," uploaded October 15, 2012, https://www.youtube.com/watch ?v=CK2O6u89A9c&feature=youtu.be.

3. Asi Burak, "Half the Sky Mobile Games on Kenyan National TV," uploaded January 5, 2013, https://www.youtube.com/watch?v=70XHdd9I8bA.

4. Nicholas D. Kristof and Sheryl WuDunn, *Half the Sky: Turning Oppression into Opportunity for Women Worldwide* (New York: Knopf Doubleday Publishing Group, 2010).

5. USAID, "Promoting Gender Equality and Access to Education," updated May 9, 2016, https://www.usaid.gov/what-we-do/gender-equality-and-womens -empowerment/addressing-gender-programming/promoting-gender.

6. USAID, "FY 2017 Budget Request Highlights," updated March 16, 2016, https://www.usaid.gov/results-and-data/budget-spending.

7. Oprah.com, "A message from Oprah," date of upload unknown, http:// www.oprah.com/world/A-Message-from-Oprah-Video.

8. PBS.org, "Half the Sky," http://www.pbs.org/independentlens/half-the -sky/.

9. Sunil Bhatia, "Op-Ed: Nicholas Kristof and the Politics of Writing about Women's Oppression in Darker Nations," *The Feminist Wire.com*, March 3, 2013, http://www.thefeministwire.com/2013/03/op-ed-nicholas-kristof -and-the-politics-of-writing-about-womens-oppression-in-darker -nations/.

10. Teju Cole, "The White-Savior Industrial Complex," *Atlantic,* March 21, 2012, http://www.theatlantic.com/international/archive/2012/03/the-white-savior-industrial-complex/254843/.

11. GSMA, "GSMA Global Mobile Economy Report 2015," June 2015, http://www.gsmamobileeconomy.com/GSMA_Global_Mobile_Economy_Report_2015.pdf.

12. Half the Sky, "Impact Report July 2014," July 2014, not available online.

13. Games for Change, "Half the Sky Movement: Multimedia Communication Initiative: An Evaluation of the 9 Minutes, Mobile Game and Video," *GamesForChange.org,* December 2012, http://www.gamesforchange.org/g4cwp/wp-content/uploads/2013/03/Half-the-Sky-Mobile-Phone-Game-Evaluation.pdf.

chapter 6

1. Mike Nizza, "Tying Columbine to Video Games," *New York Times,* July 5, 2007, http://thelede.blogs.nytimes.com/2007/07/05/tieing-columbine-to-video-games/?_r=0.

2. Steven Kent, "Game Glorifies a Life of Crime," *USA Today,* December 20, 2001, http://www.webcitation.org/6dwDKFzLe.

3. Associated Press, "Lawsuit Filed against Sony, Wal-Mart over Game Linked to Shootings," *CNN.com,* October 23, 2003, https://web.archive.org/web/20040816044256/http://edition.cnn.com/2003/LAW/10/22/videogame.lawsuit.ap/index.html.

4. Jason Schreier, "Why Most Video Game 'Aggression' Studies Are Nonsense," *Kotaku,* August 14, 2015, http://kotaku.com/why-most-video-game-aggression-studies-are-nonsense-1724116744.

5. Health.com, "Do Violent Video Games Really Cause Aggression?" August 18, 2015, http://news.health.com/2015/08/18/video-games-linked-to-aggression-psychologists-group-says/.

6. Pamela M. Kato, Steve W. Cole, Andrew S. Bradlyn, and Brad H. Pollock, "A Video Game Improves Behavioral Outcomes in Adolescents and Young Adults with Cancer: A Randomized Trial," *Pediatrics* 122 (August 2008), http://pediatrics.aappublications.org/content/122/2/e305.

7. Steven W. Cole, Daniel J. Yoo, and Brian Knutson, "Interactivity and Reward-Related Neural Activation during a Serious Videogame," *PLOS One,* March 19, 2012, http://dx.doi.org/10.1371/journal.pone.0033909.

8. HopeLab, interview with authors, April 22, 2015.
9. CDC, "Childhood Obesity Facts," last updated August 27, 2015, http://www.cdc.gov/healthyschools/obesity/facts.htm.
10. HopeLab, interview with authors, January 6, 2015.

chapter 7

1. Firas Khatib, Frank DiMaio, Seth Cooper, Maciej Kazmierczyk, Miroslaw Gilski, Szymon Krzywda, Helena Zabranska, Iva Pichova, James Thompson, Zoran Popović, Mariusz Jaskolski, David Baker, "Crystal Structure of a Monomeric Retroviral Protease Solved by Protein Folding Game Players," *Nature Structural & Molecular Biology* 18 (September 2011): 1175–1177.

2. Zoran Popovic, Foldit lead researcher, interview with the authors, April 21, 2014.

3. Oliver Sacks, "Face-Blind," *New Yorker*, August 30, 2010, http://www.newyorker.com/magazine/2010/08/30/face-blind.

4. L. Germine, R. Russell, P. M. Bronstad, G. A. M. Blokland, J. W. Smoller, H. Kwok, S. E. Anthony, K. Nakayama, G. Rhodes, and & J. B. Wilmer. "Individual Aesthetic Preferences for Faces Are Shaped Mostly by Environments, Not Genes," *Current Biology* 25 (October 2015): 1–6. http://www.lauragermine.org/articles/currentbiology_germine_inpress.pdf.

5. Laura T. Germine and Joshua K Hartshorne, "When Does Cognitive Functioning Peak? The Asynchronous Rise and Fall of Different Cognitive Abilities across the Life Span," *Psychological Science*, March 13, 2015, http://pss.sagepub.com/content/early/2015/03/06/0956797614567339.

6. David DiSalvo, "New Study Shows That Your Brain's Powers Change as You Age—Some Peaking in Your 70s," *Forbes*, March 23, 2015, http://www.forbes.com/sites/daviddisalvo/2015/03/23/new-study-shows-that-your-brains-powers-change-as-you-age-some-peaking-in-your-70s/#8c9d0a736abe.

7. Katharina Reinecke and Krzysztof Z. Gajos, "Quantifying Visual Preferences around the World," *Human Factors in Computing Systems (CHI)*, 2014, http://homes.cs.washington.edu/~reinecke/Publications_files/ReineckeCHI2014.pdf.

8. Katharina Reinecke and Krzysztof Z. Gajos, "Lab in the Wild: Conducting Large-Scale Online Experiments with Uncompensated Samples," *Proceedings of the 18th ACM Conference on Computer Supported Cooperative Work & Social Computing*, CSCW 2015: 1364–1378, http://www.eecs.harvard.edu/~kgajos/papers/2015/reinecke15labinthewild.pdf.

9. Lab in the Wild, "The First Results from the Age Guessing Experiment: How Clicking Performance Changes with Age," *Labinthewild.tumblr.com*, October 12, 2013, http://labinthewild.tumblr.com/post/63865590776 /the-first-results-from-the-age-guessing.

10. Tim Adams, "Galaxy Zoo and the New Dawn of Citizen Science," *Guardian*, March 17, 2012, https://www.theguardian.com/science/2012 /mar/18/galaxy-zoo-crowdsourcing-citizen-scientists.

11. Carolin N. Cardamone, Kevin Schawinski, Marc Sarzi, Steven P. Bamford, Nicola Bennert, C. M. Urry, Chris Lintott, William C. Keel, John Parejko, Robert C. Nichol, Daniel Thomas, Dan Andreescu, Phil Murray, M. Jordan Raddick, Anze Slosar, Alex Szalay, and Jan VandenBerg, "Galaxy Zoo Green Peas: Discovery of a Class of Compact Extremely Star-Forming Galaxies," *Monthly Notices of the Royal Astronomical Society*, July 23, 2009, http://arxiv.org/abs/0907.4155.

12. Chris Lintott, interview with the authors, January 20, 2016.

13. Chris Lintott, "Eight Years of Galaxy Zoo," *GalaxyZoo.org*, July 12, 2015, https://blog.galaxyzoo.org/tag/8thbirthday/.

14. Grant Miller, interview with the authors, February 3, 2016.

15. Mark Prigg, "Have Researchers Discovered an Alien MEGASTRUCTURE? 'Bizarre' Star Could Be Surrounded by a Dyson Sphere Built by Extraterrestrials, Researchers Claim," *Daily Mail*, October 13, 2015, http://www.dailymail.co.uk/sciencetech/article-3271546/Have -researchers-alien-MEGASTRUCTURE-Researchers-reveal-bizarre -star-say-huge-unknown-object-blocking-light.html#ixzz49grPfNpo.

16. Adam Gopnik, "Building Castles on Stars," *New Yorker*, October 30, 2015, http://www.newyorker.com/news/daily-comment/building-castles-on -stars-with-dyson-spheres.

17. Jennifer Hackett, "Computers Would Never Have Found 'Alien Superstructure' Star—It Required Citizen Science," *Scientific American*, October 21, 2015, http://www.scientificamerican.com/article/computers -would-never-have-found-alien-superstructure-star-it-required-citizen -science/?WT.mc_id=SA_SPC_20151022.

18. Jennifer Pinkowski, "How to Classify a Million Galaxies in Three Weeks," *TIME.com*, March 28, 2010, http://content.time.com/time/health/article /0,8599,1975296,00.html.

chapter 8

1. Lat Ware, "Throw Trucks with Your Mind," *Kickstarter.com*, February, 2013, https://www.kickstarter.com/projects/1544851629/throw-trucks -with-your-mind/description.

2. Megan Farokhmanesh, "Throw Trucks with Your Mind Demonstrates the Power of Calm and Focus," *Polygon*, June 8, 2013, http://www .polygon.com/2013/6/8/4366188/throw-trucks-with-your-mind.

3. Ingfei Chen, "Focusing on the Big Picture," *Science*, September 10, 2003, http://www.sciencemag.org/careers/2003/09/focusing-big-picture.

4. Stanford Center on Longevity, "A Consensus on the Brain Training Industry from the Scientific Community," October 20, 2014, http:// longevity3.stanford.edu/blog/2014/10/15/the-consensus-on-the-brain -training-industry-from-the-scientific-community/.

5. BBC, "Lumosity Brain-Training Game 'Deceived Customers,'" *BBC .com*, January 6, 2016, http://www.bbc.com/news/technology-35241778.

6. Markets and Markets, "Cognitive Assessment and Training Market Worth 7.5 Billion USD by 2020," August 2015, http://www.marketsandmarkets .com/Market-Reports/cognitive-assessment-market-1039.html.

7. Sharp Brains, "The Digital Brain Health Market 2012–2020: Web-Based, Mobile and Biometrics-Based Technology to Assess, Monitor and Enhance Cognition and Brain Functioning," January 2013, http:// sharpbrains.com/market-report/.

8. Clive Thompson, "Can Video Games Fend Off Mental Decline?", *New York Times Magazine*, October 23, 2014, http://www.nytimes.com /2014/10/26/magazine/can-video-games-fend-off-mental-decline .html?_r=3.

9. C. S. Green and D. Bavelier, "Action-Video-Game Experience Alters the Spatial Resolution of Vision," *Psychological Science* (January 2007): 88–94, http://www.ncbi.nlm.nih.gov/pmc/articles/PMC2896830/.

10. C. Shawn Green and Daphne Bavelier, "Action Video Game Modifies Visual Selective Attention," *Nature* 423 (May 29, 2003), https://www.sacklerinstitute .org/cornell/summer_institute/ARCHIVE/2003/Bavelier.pdf.

11. Michelle Trudeau, "Video Games Boost Brain Power, Multitasking Skills," National Public Radio, December 20, 2010, http://www.npr .org/2010/12/20/132077565/video-games-boost-brain-power -multitasking-skills.

12. Ravi Parikh, "Your (Smarter) Brain on Video Games: Interview with

Daphne Bavelier, Ph.D.," *MedGadget*, December 13, 2012, http://www
.medgadget.com/2012/12/your-smarter-brain-on-video-games
-interview-with-daphne-bavelier-ph-d.html.

13. J. A. Anguera, J. Boccanfuso, J. L. Rintoul, O. Al-Hashimi, F. Faraji, J.
Janowich, E. Kong, Y. Larraburo, C. Rolle, E. Johnston, and A. Gazzaley,
"Video Game Training Enhances Cognitive Control in Older Adults,"
Nature 501 (September 5, 2013): 97–101, http://www.nature.com/nature
/journal/v501/n7465/full/nature12486.html.

14. Katherine Ellison, "Video Game Is Built to Be Prescribed to Children
With A.D.H.D.," *New York Times*, November 23, 2015, http://well.blogs
.nytimes.com/2015/11/23/video-game-is-built-to-be-prescribed-to
-children-with-a-d-h-d/.

chapter 9

1. Valarie Shute, Matthew Ventura, and Robert Torres, "Formative Evaluation of Students at Quest to Learn," *International Journal of Learning and
Media* 4 (Winter 2012): 55–69, http://www.mitpressjournals.org/doi
/abs/10.1162/IJLM_a_00087?journalCode=ijlm#.V0dbS5MrKrc.

2. An initiative by The Cooney Center, E-Line Media, and Electronic
Software Association.

3. Douglas B. Clark, Emily E. Tanner-Smith, and Stephen Killingsworth,
"Digital Games for Learning: A Systematic Review and Meta-Analysis,"
SRI International, May 2013, https://www.sri.com/sites/default/files
/brochures/digital-games-for-learning-brief.pdf.

4. Lisa Bowen, "Video Game Play May Provide Learning, Health, Social
Benefits, Review Finds," American Psychological Association, February
2014, http://www.apa.org/monitor/2014/02/video-game.aspx.

5. Staff writers, "Do Educational Video Games Actually Work?" *Onlinecol-
legecourses.com,* October 23, 2012, http://www.onlinecollegecourses.com
/2012/10/23/do-educational-video-games-actually-work/.

6. Staff writers, "Globaloria: A Conversation with Dr. Idit Harel," *Markets-
forgood.org,* May 25, 2014, https://marketsforgood.org/globaloria-a
-conversation-with-dr-idit-harel/.

7. National Center for Women and Information Technology, "Globaloria:
Students Designing Educational Games (Case Study 7)," *Worlwidework-
shop.org*, October 2012, http://worldwideworkshop.org/pdfs/Globaloria
StudentsDesigningEdGames_Oct12.pdf.

8. Whitney Mallett, "Is Dys4ia a Game about the Transgender Experience or Is It a Work of Art?" *Flavorwire.com*, March 4, 2014, http://flavorwire .com/443187/the-dys4ia-debate-how-queer-creators-are-challenging -conventional-ideas-about-what-makes-a-video-game.

chapter 10

1. Robin S. Rosenberg, Shawnee L. Baughman, and Jeremy N. Bailenson, "Virtual Superheroes: Using Superpowers in Virtual Reality to Encourage Prosocial Behavior," *PLOS One*, January 30, 2013) http://vhil .stanford.edu/mm/2013/rosenberg-plos-virtual-superheroes.pdf.
2. Bjorn Carey, "NFL Commissioner Roger Goodell Steps into Virtual Reality at Stanford Lab," *Stanford.edu*, July 24, 2015, https://news .stanford.edu/2015/07/24/nfl-virtual-reality-072415/.
3. Rebecca Elliott, "Everything You Need To Know about the Ray Rice Case," *TIME.com*, September 11, 2014, http://time.com/3329351/ray -rice-timeline/.
4. Hal E. Hershfield, Daniel G. Goldstein, William F. Sharpe, Jesse Fox, Leo Yeykelis, Laura L. Carstensen, and Jeremy N. Bailenson, "Increasing Saving Behavior through Age-Progressed Renderings of the Future Self," *Journal of Marketing Research*, November 2011, http://vhil.stanford .edu/mm/2011/hershfield-jmr-saving-behavior.pdf.
5. Bank of America, "New Merrill Edge Mobile App Uses 3D Technology to Put Retirement Planning in Your Hands," *BankofAmerica.com*, February 26, 2014, http://newsroom.bankofamerica.com/press-releases/consumer -banking/new-merrill-edge-mobile-app-uses-3d-technology-put -retirement-planni.
6. Lucas Matney, "Google Cardboard Platform Picks Up Steam with 50M App Downloads to Date," *Techcrunch.com*, May 18, 2016, http:// techcrunch.com/2016/05/18/google-cardboard-platform-picks-up -steam-with-50m-app-downloads-to-date/?ncid=rss.
7. Laura Parker, "Selling Virtual Reality to the Masses," *GOOD*, March 9, 2015, https://www.good.is/articles/john-carmack-oculus-rift-vr-gdc.
8. Be Another Lab, "Gender Swap-Experiment with The Machine to Be Another," January 14, 2014, https://vimeo.com/84150219.

Index